THE BOOK OF
SOUTH BRENT

GREG WALL

HALSGROVE

First published in Great Britain in 2005

British Library Cataloguing-in-Publication Data
A CIP record for this title is available from the British Library

ISBN 1 84114 407 X

HALSGROVE

Halsgrove House
Lower Moor Way
Tiverton, Devon EX16 6SS
Tel: 01884 243242
Fax: 01884 243325
Email: sales@halsgrove.com
Website: www.halsgrove.com

Frontispiece photograph: 'Three men in a boat' –
the vicar of South Brent, Revd David Winnington-Ingram,
and his two churchwardens, Mardie Everett and Greg Wall,
set sail from Totnes to row the length of the River Dart
as a Petroctide Pilgrimage in 2003. The day ended
with a service in St Petrox Church in Dartmouth.

Printed and bound in Great Britain by CPI Bath

CONTENTS

Acknowledgements

In the 1980s I compiled the books *A Portrait of South Brent* and *South Brent and its People Remembered*. Since that time I have often been asked when the next one was coming out. Here it is! The original idea of compiling a history of the place where my family has lived for generations started back in 1969, and to list the many people who have helped and encouraged me over the years would make a volume in itself. Many of them are sadly no longer with us. Revd A.L. Vesey and Dom John Stephan, of the Order of Saint Benedict, who were instrumental in starting the whole thing off, and my mother, Mrs Sheila Wall, who acted as my 'personal assistant', will not see the publication of this third book. *The Book of South Brent* owes much to the earlier volumes and those people who helped with that must be thanked again. We have acknowledged each quotation within the text and the source of each photograph loaned to us. We hope that will be sufficient. However, I would like to thank Lord Petre of Writtle for allowing new information about his ancestors to be used, and Lucy Simister of the Mare and Foal, for displaying photographs in her shop window for several months, thus enabling the identification of many of the subjects. Finally, a special word of thanks must be given to John Giles, who worked to co-ordinate the illustrations and who was the 'critical friend' in the production of *The Book of South Brent*.

St Petroc's Church in the 1920s. Note the stone pulpit, the steps of which were moved to the vestry, the poppy-headed choir stalls and the boards beside the altar bearing the Lord's Prayer and the Ten Commandments. (Cranch Collection)

4

The east window of St Petroc's, given by Emily Bradley Elliott in memory of her husband John, lord of the manor, who died aged 24 in 1874. (McNevin Collection)

The nave of St Petroc's looking east, before the dossal curtains were removed from the altar.

The two remaining doors of the medieval rood-screen in St Petroc's.

CHAPTER 1

The Earliest Era to 1018

Alan Bennett, in his play *Habeas Corpus*, which was staged by South Brent Amateur Dramatic Society in May 1997, has his character Mrs Swabb, who was played by Carol Davis, say, 'Now a scene setting scene to set the scene and see the set, set the scene up and see the set up.' This is exactly what we must do as far as South Brent is concerned.

South Brent, or just Brent, as she is known to the locals, stands where the Avon leaves the bleak and dangerous southern Dartmoor heights and begins its journey through the tranquil South Hams. It is on the moors that the story of South Brent begins, with Bronze-Age man.

Original Brentonians

Man and his beasts have occupied Brent Moor from the earliest times. Archaeologists have found many prehistoric remains in those valleys of southern Dartmoor that lie outside the borders of the Dartmoor Forest, including that of the River Avon, often referred to by its older name, Aune. While many remains still lie undiscovered, among the largest of those in the Avon valley are Ryder's Rings at Shipley and Half Ring in the Glaze Valley. It is safe to say that the people who lived in and around them were amongst the original Brentonians. Ryder's Rings, or the Rings, lies just to the west of Long-a-traw and Ryder's Rocks and form a completely enclosed settlement measuring about 890 metres around the perimeter. It is shaped a bit like an old-

Lawn about 1950. The name of the path which runs beside the old Vicarage below Lydia Bridge derives from the river's ancient name, the Aune. Hence local people will talk about 'going down l'Aune'. It is not The Lawns.

(VERA JORDAN COLLECTION)

fashioned egg timer, the narrowest section being in the centre, and is about 335 metres from end to end. Inside there appear to have been around 30 small courtyards along the northern wall and a number of hut circles of varying sizes. One of the circles in the centre seems to have been enlarged, indicating that the site was abandoned by its original occupants only to be reinhabited soon afterwards. The only other settlement on the moor on this scale is at Grimspound, Half Ring, on the Red Brook, is smaller. There are also the remains of pounds, shelters for animals and their owners, and of hut circles and barrows, grave mounds, of stones or earth.

Agriculture has always been one of the main occupations of Brentonians, both past and present. Early man in these parts was likely to have been a pastoral rather than arable farmer, impounding his animals at Ryder's Rings and at other settlements on Brent Moor, and growing food sufficient for his needs around his home.

While the first Brentonians would have taken the raw materials of their existence from the surface of the land, as time demanded and methods became more sophisticated they began to mine it. Again it is on Brent Moor that we find the earliest industrial remains around Brent. There is evidence of Celtic tinners streaming the rivers and brooks, in particular Bala Brook. Indeed, 'Bala' derives from the word 'bal', a corruption of 'huel', the Cornish word for mining. Later, medieval tinners worked the area around Bush Pits, while others built their huts inside Ryder's Rings, the remains of which are clearly visible.

The graves of those who lived and died here abound. There are cromlechs, or dolmens, made up of three stones supporting another huge flat stone, forming a table (the Celtic words *daul* and *maen* mean 'table' and 'stone'). Longstones, or menhirs (*maen* – stone, *hir* – long), and cairns are common in the area, for example at Whitabarrow (White a burrows). The cairn on Eastern Whitaburrow stands 470 metres above sea level. Described as 'a very fine burial heap', it is circular and nearly 3.75 metres high with a base circumference of 82 metres. It is visible from all over South Devon, from Haldon in the east and from the higher points in the South Hams and Torbay. North of it lies Bishop's Meads.

In 1240 the Sheriff of Devon and 12 knights, collectively known as the perambulators, were charged with determining the boundaries between the Dartmoor Forest and the neighbouring commons.

Mrs Inez Jordan standing in the Bronze-Age remains that were flooded as the Avon Dam was filled. This photograph was taken during the drought in the summer of 1976.
(INEZ JORDAN COLLECTION)

Clive Wood sitting in the remains of the Bronze-Age buildings under the dam in the drought of 1989.
(WOOD COLLECTION)

Mrs Lodge standing by Piper's Rock on Ugborough Beacon.
(LODGE COLLECTION)

They mentioned Eastern Whitaburrow as part of their record:

to Wobroovefoot – Drylake – Crefeildfford or Dryefeild – Knattleborough – Wester Wellebrooke head – thence by Western Wellabrooke to Aune or Aven – Easter Whitaburrowe – Redlake...

To the north of Easter Head is an area known as Bloody Pool. Why it is thus named is not known, although popular belief, reinforced by the discovery of bronze 'weapons' in the area, has it that a fierce battle was fought on the site. Even with the artefacts discovered to be fishing implements and the 'blood' believed to come from local flowering plants, and though no records of a battle exist, we can never be sure that Bloody Pool was not the site of sinister events.

The pastoral farmers of pre-Christian times would have overlooked a densely wooded area to the south, while to the north was a dangerous bog.

Petroc – our First 'Hero'

It is at about this time that Petroc, our first hero, appears. A Welshman who lived in the sixth century, Petroc was a younger son of King Glywys Cernyw of Glywysing and was born about AD486. When his father died, the people of Glywysing called for Petroc to take on the crown of one the country's sub-divisions, as his brothers had done. Petroc, however, wanted to follow a religious life and so he left, with 60 followers, to study in Ireland. After about 20 years he returned to Britain and sailed into the Camel estuary in Cornwall, landing near Trebetherick. With him came three friends, Croidan, Medan and a boy named Dagan, who later became a bishop and opposed Augustine and his followers. The reception that the travellers received was far from hospitable and, on being refused water by the locals, Petroc caused a spring to appear by driving his staff into the ground.

There was already a local saint, Samson, in nearby Padstow, who, upon Petroc's arrival, set off on his own travels.

Petroc remained in the Padstow area, he and his followers establishing themselves in the Celtic monastery founded by Bishop Wethinoc at Lanwethinoc. Life in the monastery would have been ascetic, and Petroc is said to have spent much of his time sitting up to his neck in the river near Little Petherick, singing psalms.

Petroc was a missionary who travelled far and

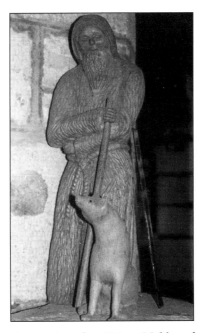

A carving by Peter Noble of St Petroc with his wolf, now in St Petroc's Church. (ADDY COLLECTION)

wide, one of his missions taking him to Rome. Legend has it that on his return journey, just as he reached Newton St Petrock in North Devon, it began to rain heavily. Although Petroc predicted that it would soon stop, the rain continued for another three days. In penance for his presumption, Petroc returned to Rome, then travelled on to Jerusalem and finally settled in India. According to legend, he was carried in a light-filled vessel to an island where he lived for seven years on a single fish that, as he ate it, constantly grew whole again. An angel then appeared to him, saying that he must return, and that there would be a wolf waiting to guide him. In Brent he is always depicted with this companion wolf. Another of his symbols is the stag. Hunted by King Constantine of Dumnonia (the Dumnonii tribe dominated the West of England for a time), the stag sought shelter with Petroc, who protected the beast and then went on to convert Constantine to Christianity.

Whatever the legend, Petroc eventually returned to Britain and made journeys in Devon and Cornwall. It is probable that during his travels Petroc came to Brent, where he founded the church which today still bears his name. It is perhaps significant that the churches dedicated to Petroc, be they in Devon or Cornwall, appear in clusters and date back to the time when he was in the area. In South Devon there are such churches at Dartmouth, at Harford and at Brent, and it is possible, as suggested by some authorities, that Petroc may have founded the original community at Buckfast. There is another cluster around Newton St Petrock itself and a line of dedications on the southern edge of Exmoor stretching as far east as Timberscombe in Somerset.

Petroc may even have travelled as far afield as Bardsey, in Wales, founding churches at St Petrox and Llanbedrog on the way.

Petroc eventually moved to Bodmin, in Cornwall, home of the hermit Guron. Guron gave up his hermitage and moved south, allowing Petroc, with the backing of King Constantine, to establish a second monastery there. Petroc became Abbot of Bodmin and eventually died on 4 June 564 at Treravel, while travelling between Little Petherick and Padstow, and was buried at Padstow.

There is evidence to suggest that the site of Brent Parish Church may have been used in pre-Christian days as a 'place of worship'. It is well known that missionaries of the period tended to adapt what they found for their own purposes, and many of

Singing Tradition – St Petroc's Church Choir

The visit of the Bishop of Exeter, Dr Robert Mortimore on 11 June 1950, St Barnabas's Day. Left to right, back row: William Knott (verger), William Cranch (churchwarden), Mr Tothill (crucifer), Bill Pinhey, Revd Ivor Jones, ?, ?, the Bishop, Reg Wright, Mark Collier, Mr Speke, Les Kidger, Mr Maundrell, John Salter; front row: George Trundle, ?, Ken Reynolds, John Wild, John Sparkes, Leonard Sparkes, Malcolm Wright, Francis Sparkes, Peter Maundrell, David Ayres. (CRANCH COLLECTION)

Choir members in the 1950s. Left to right, back row: John Wild, John Salter, Leonard Sparkes, John Sparkes; front row: George Trundle, Russell Chulk, David Ayres, Michael Wright.
(MITCHELL COLLECTION)

Choir members in the 1950s. Left to right, back row: Bertha Harley, Sarah Harley, Julie Sparkes, Ken Fox, Gillian Bishop, Alan Cox (organist and choirmaster), Ann Luker, John Salter, ?, Clive Wood, Gillian Bishop, Mrs Nancarrow, Sally Fox; seated: Mrs Dulce Campbell, Mrs Ruth Hard, Mrs Elsie Elliott, Revd A.L. Vesey (vicar 1952–71), Mrs Nell Francis, Mrs Alma Preston, Mrs Mary Vesey.

A church choir junior party, c.1990, showing David Langton (organist and choirmaster) and Richard Stevens, who subsequently also took on that role.
(CHOIR COLLECTION)

Another choir junior party, mid-1990s, this time with Dr David Precious, organist and choirmaster.
(CHOIR COLLECTION)

The church choir under David Langton. Left to right, back row: *Roger Cockings, Peter Finch, Paul Gibbons, Richard Stevens, Greg Wall;* fourth row: *Ann Anderson, Stella Gillingham, David Langton, Romola Harper, Ruth Riddell, Hilary Cockings;* third row: *Judith Morris, Clare Pecover, Cathie Pannell, Sheila Finch, Jane Tuson, Shirley Eatwell;* second row: *Robert Barclay, Michael Lewis, William Crees, Cathy Ross, Sally Wiggam, Louise Lucas, Ellen Tarr;* front row: *Gilly Ross, Paul Ferry, Amy Staddon, Romilly Everett, Rosie Ellison, Jamie Wiggam, Amanda Barclay.*

(CHOIR COLLECTION)

England's parish churches have origins in pagan graves and shrines. Petroc laid the foundation for centuries of Christian worship in Devon. It is widely recognised that where there is a Celtic dedication, then it is almost certain that it was that saint who founded the church. There are many Celtic dedications in the area, and it must be noted that the *Exeter Domesday* (*Exon*) of 1086 mentions Staverton, Stoke Gabriel, South Brent and two churches at Totnes as being attached to Buckfast Abbey. It seems that the church existed long before the revival of the cult of St Petroc within the diocese of Exeter during the fourteenth century. Whatever the case may be, Brent church existed as a small chapel at about the time Petroc was evangelising in this area. It was almost certainly a wooden structure, of which nothing would have survived. A suggestion that it may once have had some involvement in burials is supported by the discovery, in the mid-twentieth century, of bones in the Saxon part of the church (the stoke-hole) when the heating system was installed.

The Saxons arrive

When the Saxons arrived in Devon in the early years of the eighth century, much of the land had gone out of cultivation as a result of the migration of the population to Brittany. In Brent there is evidence of this in the farm name 'Yalland', which appears in a document of 1291 as 'la Yoldeland' or 'the old land', suggesting that those who named the farm recognised that it had been cultivated in the past and was not virgin land.

As we move into Saxon times we can build up a more accurate picture of what Brent was like. The base of the tower of St Petroc's Church is of Saxon origin. Indeed, quite a lot of the original building remains. The lower portion of the tower and the base of the present vestry date from this time and are at a considerably lower level than the present building, suggesting the existence of a village of sorts in this area of the parish. Anglo-Saxon villages had, in the main, two open fields around them. In this part of the world they were cultivated on an infield–outfield system. The infield, closest to the village, was cultivated almost continuously, whilst the large outfield would be partially cultivated for a few years and then let go to grazing while another area of it was put to the plough. Most authorities agree that this system disappeared very early as farmers consolidated their holdings into small fields, which would be created as follows: a tenant or farmer would, by purchase or exchange, gradually gather all his acreage together. He would then dig a trench around

St Petroc's Church from the west end, showing the tower, built in Norman times on Saxon foundations. The height of the original arches of the cruciform building can be identified on the west-facing wall of the tower. The south-facing transept is still in use as the vestry. (JAMES FORD COLLECTION)

his property, the resulting mound gradually growing as earth and stones were piled on with the successive digging of ditches and trenches. This hedge would then be topped with hazel, oak or ash, providing the poles and fuel previously gathered from the common woodland. There may even have been enough excess wood to sell. It is important to remember that this enclosing was done early on. Moving further out from the village it was not unusual to find many small farms or hamlets where farming was carried on in fields held by individuals.

One of the first written records of Brent is *The Charter of Huish*, dated AD965, in which there is mention of the Wythrom, an enclosure at Glazemeet and Pennaton Mead – possibly the enclosed hut group opposite Skitscombe Wood and Newland's Brakes. Here, beside an ancient pathway, a Saxon family would have made their home. The names that Saxon Brentonians gave to their homes tell us a lot about the kind of agriculture they engaged in and how they adapted the landscape to accommodate it. Place names ending '-ton' or '-town', '-ham' and '-coombe' suggest that the land belonging to the peasant was enclosed as fields. There are several such names in the parish, including Lutton, Splatton,

Palston, Stidston, Wonton, Pennaton, as well as the '-dons' – Stippadon, Corringdon and Staddon – and Lincombe, in the south of the parish. These endings also appear in field names – West Towne and Dinnicombes to name but two. It is interesting to note that these few examples are all close to one another, if not directly adjacent. The names ending in '-worthy' also indicate enclosure, though rather enclosure from the open moorland, Brent examples of which include Didworthy and Badworthy, both of which are on the edge of the moor. The '-ley', '-leigh', and '-beara' endings suggest the clearing of a wood which was then enclosed, for example Higher and Lower Beara, Leigh Grange, Shipley and Owley. It would seem from these names that much of the parish of Brent was enclosed from very early times, and at the beginning of the eighth century the area is one of scattered farmsteads and men working the land in comparative isolation.

So it was in these pre-Conquest days that a large part of the physical 'lie of the land' in Brent was established. This also applies to the roads and tracks throughout the parish. Right up to the north runs the Abbot's Way, reputedly the connecting track between Buckland, Buckfast and Tavistock Abbeys, although,

The view of St Petroc's Church from the weir on The Island, showing the Norman tower. This photograph was used as an Easter card from St Petroc's in 1906. (STEER COLLECTION)

as this is not the most convenient route, there is some doubt as to the validity of this idea. Another track, connecting east and west, and thus Buckfast Abbey and Plympton Priory, entered the parish via Gidley Bridge, running through Dockwell enclosures and from there following a path to Yalland. It then dropped down to the river and thence up Diamond Lane, from where it passed through some newtakes and on to Corringdon (Coryndon) Ball. From here it ran over the Glazes and on into Ugborough and Harford parishes by way of Glasscombe Corner and Spurrell's Cross. A third track comes from Aish village over Aish Ridge to the Coryndon Ball Gate and thence out across Brent Moor via Eastern Threebarrows and Knattabarrow to join the Zeal Pits Tramway. This latter is known as the 'Jobber's Path'. Bearing in mind that the 'old A38', as it now seems to have been christened, was not constructed until the

nineteenth century, we have to look to the 'Devon Lanes' to find pre-Conquest roads. The lanes that passed Glazebrook, Great Aish, and Lydia Bridge, thence to Underhill, Leigh Grange, Beara and Harbourneford, are very old indeed and tortuously follow ancient field boundaries. It is not until the end of the tenth century that the first existing written records mention Brent. In the records of Brent held by the Petre family, who acquired the manors of Brent after the Reformation, we find:

First how Kyng Edgar, yn the yere of our Lord Ixclix [AD959] have to one [...], whose name is wreten yn Danys, the said manor of Brenta, whereof the said Brent more is parsell, by his wretyng whereyn appeareth the same more bounded in Danys spech and glosed in englisshe as appeareth in the copy thereof yn the later end of the White Register Boke.

13

The First Brent Bypass

Motor Car in River: *'About 9p.m. on Tuesday a serious accident occurred at Brent Mill Bridge, South Brent, but fortunately it was not attended by serious results. An Army service car was travelling with tins of petrol towards Plymouth when it plunged 15 feet down into the river spilling about 20 cans of petrol. The driver was James Lucas and Dr Style and PS Turpin rendered all possible assistance.'*

(ANDERSON COLLECTION)

The 'new road', the A38 trunk road, was opened on 10 October 1927 by Mrs Strode, wife of the chairman of Devon County Council. It took 18 months to build at a total cost of £25,000 and the work was carried out by Wm Speight & Co. of London. Those pictured include Sgt Burrows, Misses Emma Hard and Nicey Wakeham and Mesdames Damerall, Briggs, Wakeham and Hard.

The A38 in the 1950s.

Sanderspool Cross in the 1970s.

The view of St Petroc's Church from the weir on The Island, showing the Norman tower. This photograph was used as an Easter card from St Petroc's in 1906. (STEER COLLECTION)

as this is not the most convenient route, there is some doubt as to the validity of this idea. Another track, connecting east and west, and thus Buckfast Abbey and Plympton Priory, entered the parish via Gidley Bridge, running through Dockwell enclosures and from there following a path to Yalland. It then dropped down to the river and thence up Diamond Lane, from where it passed through some newtakes and on to Corringdon (Coryndon) Ball. From here it ran over the Glazes and on into Ugborough and Harford parishes by way of Glasscombe Corner and Spurrell's Cross. A third track comes from Aish village over Aish Ridge to the Coryndon Ball Gate and thence out across Brent Moor via Eastern Threebarrows and Knattabarrow to join the Zeal Pits Tramway. This latter is known as the 'Jobber's Path'. Bearing in mind that the 'old A38', as it now seems to have been christened, was not constructed until the

nineteenth century, we have to look to the 'Devon Lanes' to find pre-Conquest roads. The lanes that passed Glazebrook, Great Aish, and Lydia Bridge, thence to Underhill, Leigh Grange, Beara and Harbourneford, are very old indeed and tortuously follow ancient field boundaries. It is not until the end of the tenth century that the first existing written records mention Brent. In the records of Brent held by the Petre family, who acquired the manors of Brent after the Reformation, we find:

First how Kyng Edgar, yn the yere of our Lord Ixclix [AD959] have to one [...], whose name is wreten yn Danys, the said manor of Brenta, whereof the said Brent more is parsell, by his wretyng whereyn appeareth the same more bounded in Danys spech and glosed in englisshe as appeareth in the copy thereof yn the later end of the White Register Boke.

13

The First Brent Bypass

Motor Car in River: '*About 9p.m. on Tuesday a serious accident occurred at Brent Mill Bridge, South Brent, but fortunately it was not attended by serious results. An Army service car was travelling with tins of petrol towards Plymouth when it plunged 15 feet down into the river spilling about 20 cans of petrol. The driver was James Lucas and Dr Style and PS Turpin rendered all possible assistance.*'

(ANDERSON COLLECTION)

The 'new road', the A38 trunk road, was opened on 10 October 1927 by Mrs Strode, wife of the chairman of Devon County Council. It took 18 months to build at a total cost of £25,000 and the work was carried out by Wm Speight & Co. of London. Those pictured include Sgt Burrows, Misses Emma Hard and Nicey Wakeham and Mesdames Damerall, Briggs, Wakeham and Hard.

The A38 in the 1950s.

Sanderspool Cross in the 1970s.

✦ CHAPTER 2 ✦

The Abbey Era, 1018–1539

The Abbey is granted the Manors of Brent

The first direct reference to owners of Brent land and assets comes in 1018, when King Canute, sometimes referred to as Cnut, the Danish king who ruled England between 1017 and 1035, together with Earl Alyward, who was of Anglo-Saxon nobility, gave the manors to the Abbot of Buckfast, shortly after the Abbey's institution. The 'manor' of Brent predates the Norman Conquest. In the Domesday Book of 1086 the modern parish of South Brent is represented by four manors: Brent, Aish, Charford and North Harbourneford, the first three of which were held by the Abbey and the fourth by William of Falaise.

The Domesday survey is an inventory and description of each of the manors of England as they were before 1066 (before the death of Edward the Confessor, on 5 January of that year), or *TRE* (*tempore Regis Edwardi*), which, in the Exeter Domesday, is rendered as 'on the day when King Edward was alive and dead'. There are two versions of the Domesday Book relevant to Devon, one being the Exchequer copy and the other the Exon version, based in Exeter, the original of which is more extensive and detailed. The survey uses men, beasts, ploughs and pence as units of assessment. The lands of the Church of Buckfast are described thus:

The Church itself holds Charford which Abbot Alwain held TRE. It paid geld for 1 hide. There is land for 8 ploughs. The abbot has 1 virgate and 1 plough in demesne, and the villeins 3 virgates and 3 ploughs. There the abbot has 7 villeins, 6 bordars, 4 serfs, 6 beasts, 44 sheep, 2 acres of meadow, and 20 acres of pasture. Formerly it was worth 20s, now 30s.

The Church itself holds Brenta. TRE it paid geld for 2 hides. There is land for 10 ploughs. The abbot has 2 hide and 1 plough in demesne, and the villeins 12 hides and 5 ploughs. There the abbot has 10 villeins, 8 bordars, 5 serfs, 14 beasts, 55 sheep, 5 acres of wood-land, 4 of meadow and 30 of pasture. Formerly worth 30s; now it is worth 40s.

The Church itself holds Brente. TRE it paid geld for 2 hides. There is land for 6 ploughs. Thereof the abbot has 2 hide and 2 plough in demesne, and the villeins 11 hides and 3 ploughs. There the abbot has 8 villeins, 6 bordars, 4 serfs, 11 beasts, 70 sheep, 30 goats, wood(land) 1 league in length by 1 furlong in breadth. In demesne is half a plough and 4 slaves; 8 villeins and

6 bordars with 3 ploughs. Formerly it was worth 20s; now 30s.

In addition:

Reginald holds HARBOURNEFORD from William (of Falaise). Alric held it in TRE and it paid geld for half a hide. There is land for 4 ploughs. There are 3 villans and 2 bordars with 1 slave have 1 plough. There are two acres of meadow and 4 of woodland. Formerly 8s it is now worth 10s.

William of Falaise also held Holne, Dean Prior, Rattery and Dartington.

The fact that the survey quotes a large number of sheep shows just how important the production of wool was as a source of income for the Abbey.

Not all the units used in the survey were uniform and care must be taken in working out the size of villages from this source.

The population of Brent in the survey consisted of villeins, serfs and bordars. All these men lived on demesne land and paid dues to the lord. The dues might be in the form of work or even goods in kind. We notice that there are no freemen, which is quite characteristic of this part of the world.

The late Dom John Stephan of Buckfast Abbey formulated the following population figures for the four manors from the Domesday survey:

	Villeins	Serfs	Bordars	Total
Brent	10	5	8	23
Aish	8	4	6	18
Charford	10	5	8	23
North Harbourneford	3	1	2	6
				70

These figures represent the number of families in the four manors. A family would average about four people, so the total population of the four manors, the modern parish of Brent, would have been about 280 souls. When we compare this with the four Domesday towns of Devon we find that Brent's total population of 280 puts Brent on a par with them.

Exeter	*2,000*
Totnes	*500*
Lydford	*350*
Barnstaple	*270*
South Brent	*280*

In 2000 an Ecumenical Flower Festival, held in South Brent's three churches simultaneously, had the theme 'The Light of the World'. The arrangements here, in St Dunstan's Roman Catholic Church, represented (clockwise from top right): The Vatican, Portugal, Italy, Easter and Poland.

However, despite being connected to the important Abbey of Buckfast, South Brent, because of its scattered geography, never attained the status suggested by its population size in the eleventh century. Two of the manors, 'Brenta' and 'Brente', represent Brent and Aish, while Charford and North Harbourneford are some miles distant, in the south and east of the present parish.

The Medieval Scene

We know that in 1247 the village of Brent consisted of the church and seven houses. These are the very old buildings that surround St Petroc's Church, most notably Church House and Island House. It is interesting to observe that the village lies off what would have been a main crossroads where Fore Street is now. Some time before 1246 the west and north transepts of the older church were pulled down and the ground level of the church rose. Looking inside the base of the present tower, you will see that the tops of the arches are very low. To reach the original ground level, such as can be found in the old stoke-hole, it is necessary to go several metres below the present ground level to that of the surrounding fields on the south side on the churchyard. The base of the Saxon church was used as the foundation for the new building, constructed with a single nave and two outer bays. Described as square and pinnacled, the tower is widely considered to be one of the finest Norman examples in the county. The font, dating from the same period, is still in use in 2005. But what did the village surrounding the church look like?

When we were at school in days gone by we were taught that, in the Middle Ages, villages in England were farmed using a system of three large fields divided into strips which were distributed amongst the villagers. We have already discussed the probability that Saxon Brent, and for that matter Aish and Charford, were cultivated on an infield–outfield system that was consolidated into smallholdings very early on.

Professor Maitland, in his book *Domesday Book and Beyond*, puts forward the view that the typical medieval nuclear village of houses, church, mill, etc., surrounded by three or four large fields subdivided into strips, was not at all common in the hilly terrain of Devon and Cornwall, where the Celtic influence was stronger. Here, manors would consist of scattered farmsteads with their own fields, just as those at Dean Prior and Harford remain to this day.

Other authorities maintain that in the South West the typical method of cultivation involved the use of an infield and an outfield, as discussed in Chapter 1.

Where might these two fields have been? If we take a bird's-eye view of the immediate surroundings of the church and ignore the cuttings and other man-made changes brought about by the construction of the railway station, we find a comparatively level area of terrain which stretches from 'Headlands', a small farm on the last flat terrain before the land begins to rise to Brent Hill, through to Church Street. It is interesting to note that a 'headland' was the pathway left unploughed in a communal field to let ploughs and carts get to the strip in the middle. They also gave the farmer room to turn his plough easily. At the bottom of Church Street the road turns almost at a right angle and then runs more or less directly to Headlands, where it bears left to go on to Lydia Bridge and to Lutton. The eastern parallel, from Fore Street, runs up along Hillside before it goes on out of the parish, along the old main road. This could well be the site of the 'northfield' or outfield.

On the south side of Church Street is a very old property called Southfields. Archaeologists suggest that there is evidence of some form of strip cultivation in this area of the village. The 1842 tithe map shows that all the fields run parallel to each other along the south side of Church Street, Totnes Road and the northern end of Plymouth Road, suggesting that they were formed from consolidated strips. This area, therefore, might well have been the infield.

Buckfast Abbey, which owned Brent and Buckfast manors in the Middle Ages, was one of the Cistercian houses of England, and the Cistercians were great sheep farmers. Pastoral farming has always been important in the area and enclosure was connected with it. The production and processing of wool affected the prosperity and population of neighbouring Buckfastleigh in the nineteenth century – indeed, the Cistercian monks of Buckfast were often accused, rightly or wrongly, of eating away at the rights of the commoner on Dartmoor with their sheep farming. After the Dissolution of Buckfast Abbey there is frequent reference to 'parcells' of land in the Petre records. These 'parcells', many of whose names end in 'park', had a fixed acreage, and it is reasonable to assume that they had existed for many

The Norman font, made of red sandstone, in St Petroc's Church. The decoration has a honeysuckle motif with a cable twist around the top of bowl and a Norman dog-tooth pattern at the bottom, a design reputed to have come from the Middle East. The cover is modern and was made by Mr Jack Ainscow, a member of the congregation, in about 1980. (MALE COLLECTION)

An aerial view of South Brent in 1939 clearly showing the communities of South Brent and Brent Mill as separate entities. The regular fields in the centre show the last vestiges of the medieval infield, where strips have been consolidated to make enclosures. They are surrounded by the meadowlands leading down to the river. Compare the shape of these fields to the much older, irregular, ones at the top of the photograph. (AEROFILMS LTD)

years. The suffix 'park' refers to enclosure which, Dr Finberg suggests, indicates the consolidation of holdings from open fields. These 'parks' surround every hamlet community in the parish and are commonly mentioned in the Petre leases. Local man Don Stansbury has made a study of the field names as found on the tithe map, many of which, to the north of Church Street and Totnes Road, are 'parks' – Bottom Park, Furze Park, Roper's Park, Inner, Greater and Little Palstone Parks and Pool Park, to name but a few. In the Southfields area are Higher and Lower Rack Park – associated with wool production, as well as with orchards, and names such as First Field, Second Field, Third Field and even Pack Horse Field, beyond which are meadows stretching down to the river. At Didworthy on 30 April 1631, John Thome was granted the following:

Premises: house formerly called the kitchen within courtelage of Dydworthie tenement with cellar adjoining, stable, wainhouse, easter barn and easter garden with herb garden adjoining Easter Meadow alias Cornerparke, closes called Westernose alias Westernhalf Easter Littell Parke, Short Furlonge, Furseparke, West Towne with Brodea parke.

A furlong refers to a set of strips within an open field, again associated with enclosure. Many plots are mentioned as being closes of barton or demesne land.

The 'typical nuclear medieval village' has a mill belonging to the lord of the manor. The oldest mill in South Brent, and also the last mill to close down, is Manor Mills at Brent Mill. As the name suggests, it originated as the lord's customary mill to which the tenants of the lord of the manor had, as part of their rent, to bring their crops to be ground. Indeed, as early as 1277 mention is made of the need to bring corn from Bullhornstone to the Manor Mill for grinding. Although, the principal mill in the area, it was a long way from Brent. By later medieval times there were two closer mills, one at Millswood and one at the end of L'Aune path by the present railway bridge. At Brent Mill are such field names as Higher and Lower Mill Park, Mill Meadow and the Longfield.

A look back at the bird's-eye view maps suggests that a series of hamlets surrounded areas that were quickly consolidated into smallholdings. One is centred on the church, one around the mill at Brent Mill and, in later medieval times, one at the 'crossroads', now Fore Street, where the oldest hostelry in Brent, the Pack Horse, is to be found. Then there are the ancient communities of Aish, Didworthy, Lutton, Harbourneford and Charford, familiar to us in some respects today. Nevertheless, by the fourteenth century, with the support of the Abbey of Buckfast, Brent was to become a market town and an economic centre of some importance.

Dom Adam Hamilton describes how the people of Brent lived their lives:

The villeins of Brent owned their homesteads and lands almost by hereditary descent and their oxen and ploughs were their own property. The bordars, or cottagers usually possessed no oxen. The serfs, few in number were, as Bishop Brownlow puts it, 'fast becoming merged in the cottier class above them'. Voluntary manumissions were frequent; if the lord made one of his bondmen work on a Sunday, he became a freeman.

Brent was a valuable asset for the Abbey. During the incumbency of first named vicar of Brent, Richard de Teygnmuive (Teignmouth), appointed in 1268, Brent was given the right to have its own gallows and to check the standard of beer brewed through the right of 'assize of beer', granted by Stanborough Hundred in 1274. In 1288 Pope Nicholas IV launched his taxation decree to support a crusade that King Edward I wished to undertake. All churches and religious houses had to support this to a level of ten per cent of their value. The value of the church in Brent was £6.13s.4d., the tenth part of which came to 13s.4d., whilst the vicarage paid 30s. The Abbey itself paid 10s.8d., while Buckfastleigh escaped the levy completely. Brent seems to have been very prosperous. Sometime between 1289 and 1296 Gervoise succeeded Richard of Teignmouth as vicar of South Brent.

Sir John Durant was installed as vicar of South Brent in 1337. It is claimed that Sir John, third named vicar, was recorded in 1340 as being a 'poor priest'. The poor priests of the fourteenth century were graduates of Oxford and followers of John Wycliffe, and were sent out to preach the Gospel of Jesus Christ.

They lived in poverty, journeying about the country clad in simple russet and preaching as the Dominicans had done; later, some, if not most, of them were laymen. How Sir John became an incumbent is not known.

The Start of the Fair

The year 1350 marks a zenith in the history of South Brent. In this year King Edward III (1327–77) granted a royal charter to Abbot Philip Beaumont of Buckfast giving the abbot and his successors the right to hold a three-day fair at Michaelmas on Brentedoune, i.e. between the village and Brent Hill – the outfield. Brent was the richest of the Abbey manors, and the most populous. Dom Adam Hamilton writes in his *History of St Mary's Abbey of Buckfast*, published in 1906:

On Brent Down in Abbot Philip's time, the sellers set up their booths; itinerant jugglers and musicians came to ply their vocation; and we learn with regret from Bishop Grandisson, that the ale sometimes flowed too freely, with the usual results, on such occasions.

Fairs were not so much for buying and selling of stock, etc., as for the buying of stores that would last until the next year. Cloth was sold, as well as spices, seed and corn – indeed, anything not sold at the weekly market. It was also a time of gaiety and great festivity. It is quite possible, because of the Black Death of 1348–50, that the first ever Michaelmas Fair was not held until a couple of years after this. Sir John Durant, vicar of Brent at the time, was a likely victim of this terrible scourge, which was responsible for the decimation of England's population. Though the people of the village perhaps had to wait for their first fair, doubtless when Abbot Philip came to open it there would have been much celebration. In 1788 the date of the fair was moved to the three days beginning on the last Tuesday in September.

Part of the celebration would have taken place in St Michael's Chapel, which stood on the summit of Brent Hill. The late Dom John Stephan, OSB, found evidence to confirm this. In the registers of Bishop Brantyngham for 1374, the following Latin entry has been found:

Item, ibidem (Chawleigh) xxiiij die mensis (Augusti), Dominus Concessit Licenciam Abbati Buckfestri, quod possit INSINGULIS FESTIS SANCTI MICHAELIS, necnon in majoribus festis, in capella sua de Brentedoune celebrare, et per presbyteros ydoneos in sua vel Confratrum suorum, ac cuiuslibet ipsorum, presentia facere celebrari quandui Domino Placuerit duraturam.

This is from a charter giving permission to celebrate a mass in the Abbot's Chapel on Brent Hill on St Michael's Day. It is interesting to note that the chapel is not to be used on any other day. That the mass and fair were held on the same day leads us to suppose that they were connected. The chapel was otherwise used as a public oratory and was not a rival to St Petroc's. This still happens in modern European countries. The same building probably saw yet another use, as Brent Hill formed an important link in the chain of beacons lit to warn of the approach of the Spanish Armada.

We need not, however, refute a story dating from the eighteenth century of Mr Tripe, an Ashburton man who, in order to amuse himself, is reputed to have built a windmill on the summit of Brent Hill, which he could see from his house in Ashburton. It is likely that rather than building a complete mill he simply attached sails to what was already there – the ruins of Saint Michael's Chapel. In 1777 the chapel was struck by lightning. It is interesting to note that not until the following year was the date of the fair changed.

Sir John Monlisle was installed as vicar of South Brent in 1349 and was succeeded in 1355 by Benedict Riche who, in the same year, was appointed confessor for the Archdeanery of Totnes.

Robert Knyght's Enormities

During the reign of Richard II (1377–99) Robert Knyght was appointed by Abbot Robert Simons of Buckfast as the vicar of South Brent. Henry II had confirmed rights, granted by Henry I and their Anglo-Saxon predecessors, for fishing on the River Avon. A dispute arose between the abbot and the vicar involving John Fox, John Beare, William Ffenford, William Pitman, William and John Langdon, and Walter and Thomas Schaghe, some of the abbot's tenants. In 1392 the men were accused of breaking into the abbot's close at South Brent, with force and arms, and of destroying his young fruit trees and encroaching on his reserved fishery, from which they took fish and other goods and chattels to the value of £20. The fish consisted of 40 salmon, as well as many perches, eels and 'seafish'. They also went into his rabbit warren and took 500 conies worth 100 shillings, besides ruining his pasture land, also worth 100 shillings, and committing 'other enormities'. In all, the damage inflicted on the abbot amounted to at least £100.

Some of the defendants claimed that the abbot had frequently employed them to catch fish for him in the same part of the river, while the vicar declared that he had been the abbot's chaplain, and had caught two conies for the abbot's table with the abbot himself. All the defendants denied ever having used force or violence in their transgressions. Moreover, they had already been punished by the abbot for any damage caused him, and had given satisfaction. They denied damaging his trees and plantations, though they did admit to having carried away 12 oak trees, and to having helped themselves to some 20 rabbits. They argued that the extent of their 'depredations' could not amount to more than £10 in money value. Even though the abbot declared the matter settled, Robert Knyght was still sent to Flete Prison for reasons not explained. Eventually, after dragging on for years, and after a retrial, errors in the case led to the defendants being acquitted.

The next two incumbents of the parish were John Junne (1406–27), and Master Edmund Fychet (1427–28).

A Crime Most Sacrilegious

By 1436 we know from an incident that happened at the end of Corpus Christi vespers in that year that the Parish Church was very much its present shape – indeed, parts of it today would probably still be recognised by fifteenth-century Brentonians. For reasons unknown, one Thomas Wake (or Weke) dragged the vicar, Master John Hay, who had been appointed in 1428, dressed in full vestments, from the altar and through a small doorway and, with the help of some accomplices, beat him to death. Apart from Canterbury Cathedral, Brent is believed to be the only place in England where this has happened. The blocked remains of the doorway can still be made out.

The records of September 1436 tell us that the Bishop of Exeter dedicated three altars in the church after the murder of Hay. The altar in the north aisle was dedicated to St Mary the Virgin (i.e. a Lady Chapel), the altar in the south aisle to St Margaret and St Catherine and the main altar to St Petroc.

The list of incumbents continues:

1436	*Sir John Ufforde is installed as Vicar*
1441	*Sir John Frenshe*
1452	*Sir David Frenshe*
1461	*William Jemse*
1469	*William Feyer*
	William Hale
1498	*John Drake*
1510	*Robert Barber*
1516	*Walter Southcote*

Brent Hill Pilgrimage

The ruins of St Michael's Chapel on the summit of Brent Hill in 1860.
(CRANCH COLLECTION)

Below: *Brent Hill Pilgrimage in the late 1990s. Revd Michael Malsom introduced the custom of taking crosses to the summit of Brent Hill in 1972. This has taken place every year since then on Good Friday, the only exception being in 2001, the year of the foot and mouth epidemic. Although originally three crosses were taken up in the ecumenical pilgrimage, this has now become one. The event continues to draw a large 'congregation', even in wind and sleet.*

The medieval Church House, as painted by local artist Christine Raikes.

The valley above Shipley Bridge. (CRANCH COLLECTION)

Picturesque South Brent – the cottages at Lydia Bridge.

The footpath from Lutton to Headlands. (FORD COLLECTION)

The New Church House, 1517

It is recorded on 3 June 1517 in an indented feoffement that Abbot Alfred Gyll (1512–25) gave to John Ferris senr, Robert Porford, Roger Hengiston, John Deyman of Palston, John Thorne, William Allman, Edward Saunder senr and John Stidston of Coryngdon:

[a] parsel of land lying between the Abbey's tenement in which Thomas Yolland lives on the south, their tenement which John Symon, weaver holds on the North, their garden which John Mychell holds on the east and the King's street on the west.

They received it to hold for the building of a new house, called a church house, the rents and profits from which were to be used for the maintenance of the Parish Church and its ornaments.

Abbot Gyll was also given a licence in 1521 'to hold weekly market at Buckfastleigh and two fairs annually of three days each at South Brent.' This would seem to be a confirmation of the existing fairs rather than a new grant, but is nonetheless notable since Abbot Gyll's abbacy was rather more eventful than it might have been in that he was called to task for breeches of regulations set down by the Cistercian authorities.

John Leland and the *Valor Ecclesiasticus*

John Leland, who surveyed monastic libraries before the Dissolution, and who was one of the early travellers in Devon, on passing through the parish in about 1540, records:

From Modbyri to the Forde wher I passed over Awne Ryver about 4. or 5. miles. This water cummith by Estbrenton, and a little lower even by the Toun, is a bridge over Aune. Estbrenton is in the highwat betwixt Plymouth and Excestre.

At the time of the *Valor Ecclesiasticus*, which listed the value of all monastic lands prior to the Dissolution of the Monasteries by Henry VIII, South Brent was the richest of the Abbey manors, and was valued at £121.6.7¾d. Of this, £87.16.3d. came from customary dues, with various other dues making up the rest. The long association between South Brent and Buckfast Abbey was now almost at an end.

21

Bridges of South Brent

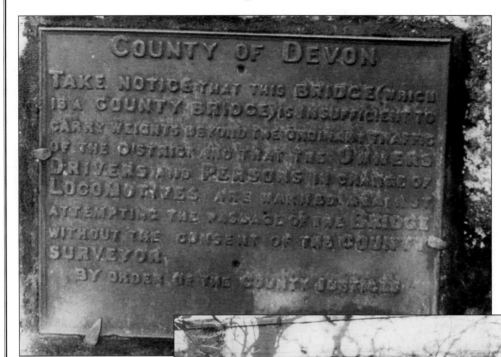

The nineteenth-century weight restriction notice at Lydia Bridge.
(CLAMP COLLECTION)

The railway bridges at the end of L'Aune path. They were constructed side by side when the railway was made into a double track in the 1890s.

Didworthy Bridge.

CHAPTER 3

The Petre Era, 1539–1826

Sir William Petre, the first secular lord of the manor of Brent since 1018. He bought the manors after the Dissolution of Buckfast Abbey. Devon born, he served four Tudor monarchs without coming to grief.

(REPRODUCED BY KIND PERMISSION OF LORD PETRE OF WRITTLE)

'England's First Civil Servant'

On 25 February 1538, the Abbot of Buckfast, Gabriel Donne, surrendered his monastery to Henry VIII. From that day until 5 July 1546, the manor of Brent was the property of King Henry. On the latter date Sir William Petre became lord of the manor, and with it acquired the right to appoint the vicars of the parish. He was granted the manor by the king, partly in exchange for property in Warwickshire and Oxfordshire, and partly for services rendered. On 16 March 1547 he purchased the manor of Brent Moor from Sir Thomas Denys of Holcombe Burnell.

Sir William Petre was born in the early years of the sixteenth century, in 1500 or 1505, at Tornewton, near Torbryan, the son of John and Alice Petre. He married twice, fathered nine children and was to serve four Tudor monarchs. He first came to royal notice as tutor to George Boleyn, Viscount Rochford. He became Thomas Cromwell's proctor, or assistant, in 1535 and was the visitor to the monastic houses of southern England prior to the Dissolution. His job was to draw up an inventory of the possessions of

each abbey and persuade its abbot and chapter to surrender their abbey to the king, and was present when Abbot Gabriel Donne surrendered the Abbey of Buckfast. Despite his being instrumental in and benefiting from the destruction of the monasteries in England, he was exonerated by Pope Paul IV and, on condition that he build almshouses for the poor, was not included in the Interdict of Excommunication. He carried out this obligation at Ingatestone, near to his home, Ingatestone Hall, which remains the Petre family home.

Sir William was knighted in 1543 when he became Secretary of State and a Privy Councillor. In 1545, he served as ambassador to Emperor Charles V. What is remarkable about Sir William is that he served four of the Tudor monarchs – Henry VIII, Edward VI, Mary I and Elizabeth I – throughout the turbulent Reformation without losing his head. His discretion and experience were his redeeming qualities, and the French diplomat, the Duke de Chatillon described him as 'the man who said nothing'. Sir William, who has been described as 'England's first civil servant', retired from the service of Queen Elizabeth I in 1557 and remained at Ingatestone, where he died on 13 January 1571.

William began to purchase property in Devon in about 1540, the family already owning much in Gloucestershire and Somerset. As well as at Brent, they held other properties in Devon, including Hole in Blackawton parish (at least until 1606), the manors of Churchstow and Herberton, the manor and borough of Kingsbridge, Higher Fleet in East Allington and Kellench of Torbryan, not to mention considerable property in East Devon. Most of the property owned by the Petres consisted of land and the advowsons that went with it, although they did hold the parsonage of St Giles in the Wood in West Devon.

William's son, Sir John, was created Baron Petre of Writtle in 1603, 31 years after his father's death. None of the heads of the family ever lived at Brent, the whole of the western estate being administered under a manorial framework by stewards living in the area. The benevolent squire did not play much of a part in the history of Brent at this time.

In 1550 Philip Phrear became vicar of South Brent. The living was confirmed with him on 5 May 1559.

Under the hand and seale of James Bp of exon. Confirmed by the Dean and Chapt. Under seale. Assented to by Sr Wm. Petre under his hand and seale.

The manorial court of 17 November 1913. The members of the manorial court and children from Brent Board School outside Cranch's shop, now the pharmacy, before the annual bread-weighing and ale-tasting ceremony.

(CRANCH AND INEZ JORDAN COLLECTIONS)

Ratified, approv'd & confirm'd by Philippus Phrear Vicar of So Brent, under his hand and Seale.

The evidence appears in the *Book of Evidences* from Christ Church (the spelling is original).

The Endowment and Settlement of the Vicarige of South Brent, by which is given to the Vicar there the parsonage of the Parish Church of Brent, with all and singular tithes, rights and emolumts, as well spiritual as temporal; & that Philip Phrear the Vicar may take possession thereof to hold under these condicions following;

The Vicar to pay to the Dean and Chapt one annual & ppetual rent of 20£ at this Cathrdral Church at the feasts of Th'anuntacon and St. Mich by even porcons.

Various penalities then follow for late payment of dues.

Every vicar presented to the vicarage was also required to pay £3.6s.8d. to the dean and chapter of Christ Church within one year, with the inevitable penalties for non payment.

'When Good King Hal had Reigned Awhile'

It is certain that in Tudor times the Parish Church, the Church House, Island House, probably the Pack Horse and the Anchor Hotel, as well as the toll-house were much the same as they are today. In addition we know that at the top end of Church Street was Cheape House, standing on pillars and with an open ground floor. It is likely that markets and village trading went on around this building. Most Elizabethan Brentonians would have lived in stone-built cottages considerably more rough and ready than the white-washed, half-timbered buildings we are used to seeing in pictures of Elizabethan towns such as Totnes. Brent was not a place to attract merchants and those who built such houses. Most of the outlying farms were already old in Tudor times.

Palston, Beara, Yalland and Wonton would all have been familiar to sixteenth-century Brentonians. Stidston Farm was at this time held by the Cholwich family and consisted of 100 acres of land, Andrew Cholwich also holding land in neighbouring parishes. At the same time, John Furze owned three houses in the area, as well as ten acres of arable land, four of meadow, six of pasture and areas of furze and heath at Pennaton. Furze Park once belonged to him and he also held land in Dinnicombes. All of this land was worth £3 each year.

As mentioned in Chapter 2, in 1588 Brent Hill served as a beacon to warn of the coming Spanish Armada, providing the link between Ugborough Beacon to the west, where the message would have come via Penn and Fire Down, and Buckfastleigh and Dean Prior, from where the message would spread eastwards. These beacons were constantly attended and a watch kept in case the warning came. The danger was of a false alarm, for example mistaking a fire on the moors for the beacon – such a misinterpretation would have caused enormous uproar.

It has long been rumoured that a network of underground passageways links many of the old farms, although there is no evidence to support this. Also without foundation is the theory that the Church House was a nunnery, although many priest holes have been found in the outlying farms.

Borough or Not?

It is in this period that one of the great puzzles concerning South Brent begins. It is epitomised in a poem written by Mrs E. Catt in 1920:

On the progress of Brent, 1920

South Brent is a 'Town' learnt so at school
Though a village it's called by most as a rule.
A beautiful church, a beautiful school
Beautiful air and scenery as well.
With the telephone service few can compete,

And parishioners' exhibits at shows hard to beat
A playing field is wanted so let's make this endeavour
Knowing full well 'twill give little ones pleasure.
And when that takes place we shall proudly say
South Brent is a town not a village today.

Historically, South Brent was always referred to as a town, although everyone has their own opinion as to what constitutes a town. At the beginning of the Petre era Brent is first referred to as a borough. Some historians doubt very much that it was, although there is some evidence to support the claim. The following quotation is from a 1904 newspaper report:

From the reign of Philip and Mary in 1556, South Brent has held its charter as a properly constituted borough. Furthermore, the borough is governed by the Lord of the Manor and the Court Leet, the Court Baron and the jurymen of the parish.

It is interesting to note that at this time Sir William Petre was in the service of Queen Mary I and highly thought of, so it is possible that he had some influence over his royal mistress. The report goes on to describe the events of the Court Leet: 'The borough still holds and uses the old beam and scales for bread-weighing, and quart and pint cups for ale-tasting.'

These implements were used by the bread-weighers who read the king's declaration, as that of the lord of the manor, and then demanded bread from the bakers in order that they might check its weight. Similarly, the ale-tasters tested the beer from the victuallers of the parish. This ceremony still goes on in the neighbouring town of Ashburton. The report lists the names of all the officials: W. Pearse, portreeve; J. Veale, reeve and bailiff; P. Blight and H. Veale, ale-taster and bread-weigher respectively; J. Bunker, town crier and assistant bread-weigher and J. Stanbury, scavenger with the jurymen of South Brent. These men had held traditional positions of authority in the manor from time immemorial and were not appointed merely as tradition demanded. The Courts Leet and Baron were, along with the Court Customary and Hall Moot, responsible for all local government and justice on the manor. They were, in fact, the main organs of local government in medieval England. In South Brent both the Courts Leet and Baron met triennially and at every meeting, including those within living memory, the borough charter was produced and read at the commencement of the proceedings. It was read out by the lord of the manor, acting in his capacity as the equivalent of the Mayor. The Courts Leet and Baron could then carry out their official duties.

A further reference to Brent as a borough appears in the Petre leases, held in the County Record Office. On 2 August 1639 a lease was granted to Symon Shepard of South Brent 'for all fairs and markets within the town and borough of Brent and drift of Brente Moore.'

In 1789 William Foot, in signing the 'Ringers' Book', the official record of the annual election of bell-ringers at St Petroc's Church, is described as 'Mayor of Brent'.

You must judge for yourself in this matter. One suggestion often put forward is that South Brent is one of the 'failed boroughs' of Devon, which, although granted borough status by their lords, were not officially recognised as such.

Brent's Mills Expand

The River Avon is a fast-flowing moorland river most of the time and as such is an important source of water-power. There have been no less than five working water-mills along the banks of the Avon between Lutton and Brent Mill, the highest at Crackhills, with the next, Lydia Mill, just below Lydia Bridge. Another lay at the other end of L'Aune path and then came Millswood, Manor Mill being the last one at Brent Mill. They were all served by a series of leats, either individual or shared.

In the mid-sixteenth century the Thorne family were the millers at Manor Mill, which remained in their hands for over 100 years. In 1605 it was held by James and Elizabeth Thorne, who paid £5.12s.8d. in rent. By 1664, when Thomas Millman took over, another mill had been built – William Thorne, son of James and Elizabeth, had put in another water grist mill and constructed a dwelling-house. The Millman

The mill below the railway bridge at the end of L'Aune path. (CRANCH COLLECTION)

A general view of South Brent at the turn of the nineteenth century before any of the estates were built. Millswood Mill is very prominent on the right and the railway station is on the left.

family were still in occupation in 1696, although the original Thomas and his wife, Agnes, had died. A second Thomas, a mercer from Ashburton, took over the lease, but before the lease was sealed the mills accidentally burned down. Like the Maddocks at Lydia Mill, however, Thomas Millman built them again at a cost of £150 and a new lease was signed. The mill then passed through several hands. Between 1766 and 1770 the miller was Philip Goodman, followed for a short time by Samuel Ryder.

The earliest reference we have to Lydia Mill comes in the 1580 survey of the Petre estates in Devon, where it is described as a fulling mill, a fuller being someone who cleans and thickens cloth. The mill's leat ran into the river through a sluice 45 metres downstream from the wheel. Henry Maddock took over Lydia Mill on 30 April 1622 and used it as a grist or flour mill. In addition to paying a nominal rent of 10s., he had to maintain the mill with two suitable millstones and the tackling that went with them. The next reference to the mill appears in about 1669, when it was destroyed by a flood. Not to be defeated by such a disaster, Maddock rebuilt it at his own cost, and a new lease appears for this second building in the same year. At the turn of the century the mill was still in the Maddock family, in the shape of Henry's grandson, to whom a lease was granted in 1695. As with most of Brent's mills, Lydia Mill has often changed use, becoming a wheelwright's shop and forge which, in the nineteenth century was worked successively by Mr Langler and Mr Vinnicombe in a time when the sight of carts, wheels and suchlike,

and the craftsmen who dealt with them, was commonplace. Much trade must have been had from Crackhills mill across the road. Lydia Mill is now a dwelling-house and, although the wheel no longer functions, it can still be seen.

Both Millswood and Manor Mills (the latter being at Brent Mill and the last one in use), were worked by the same leat, which took water from the second weir below the church. The top sluice, still visible in 2005, controlled the amount of water in the leat.

In the seventeenth century Millswood was operated as a teazle mill by Henry Wellinge, a fuller. Rock Park, at that time known as Rack Park, was the field in which the fulling racks were kept, and there were lime pits connected with the mill on The Island. The mill was taken over by Henry's son, William Wellinge, on whose death in 1691 it passed to his daughters, Anne and Joan. Although themselves millers, because they were fullers they were still required to have their corn ground at the lord of the manor's customary mill, Brent Mill.

'A Notorious Delinquent'

John Gandy was installed as vicar of South Brent in 1627 and was the incumbent at a very turbulent time – the Civil War. He was chaplain to the Bishop of Salisbury and very anti-Puritan, which in itself was to be the cause of great distress for him and his family. In 1642, his prebendal stall at Torleton was sequestrated and given to one Britten, a Parliamentarian. Prebendary Gandy was living at Brent at the time.

At about the time that John Gandy came to Brent, a Puritan preacher, Christopher Jellinger, arrived in this country. Jellinger was born early in the seventeenth century near the city of Worms, famous as the place where, in the previous century, Martin Luther had posted on the church door his famous 95 theses against the Roman Catholic Church. Revd Jellinger is reported to have been a very 'ardent' student who studied at universities in Germany and Switzerland. He held Puritan views and became a member of the Calvinist community in Geneva before coming to this country at the request of Mr White of Dorchester. Soon afterwards he went to Exeter, where he was supported by the Puritan Bishop Hall, and then moved to Totnes. In 1631 he married Agnes Hayne, a widow from West Allington, and efforts were made to find him a living in Devon.

John Gandy, because of his anti-Puritan views, had become unpopular with some of the people of Brent, who presented a petition to Parliament reporting that he was a 'notorious delinquent and that his vicarage should be sequestered'.

In 1644, as John Gandy was going to church, he was arrested and forced to walk to Dartmouth dressed in all his robes and carrying a Bible in his hand. Frequently threatened by his captors, he was held prisoner until he paid £100 ransom. He then travelled to London to try to gain some influence there, leaving Mrs Gandy in Brent Vicarage. In his absence his house was ransacked and his wife and family thrown out of house and home to beg or starve. It is ironic that not only had Gandy's father helped Christopher Jellinger when he first arrived in Exeter, but that the soldier figuring most prominently in the ejection of Mrs Gandy was a man whose debts she had recently paid, thus freeing him from prison. Revd Gandy was later dispossessed of his living and, while in London, was forced to sell his books to provide enough money on which to live.

From 1642, the living was held by Christopher Jellinger, although it seems that despite petitions in Parliament that 'Christopher Jellinger shall be Vicar of South Brent in the County of Devon' there is no evidence that this position was ever officially confirmed. When Jellinger was ejected under the Bartholomew Act, Gandy was restored, and remained vicar until 1672. On his death he was buried in the Lady Chapel. Christopher Jellinger, who lived to an old age, died at Kingsbridge in 1685.

Educating the Young

There has been provision for the education of the ordinary people of South Brent since John Petre left £70 per annum from income from his property in Cornworthy. A customer of Exeter, he died in 1570 and was buried in Brent Church. The first mention of a schoolmaster in Brent appears after the Restoration of King Charles II in l660. Teachers at that time were required to be licensed by the Diocesan Bishop, which at least provided some guarantee of conformity and loyalty. In Brent one such licensed teacher was Stephen Kellond, described as 'a cavalier in the late wars, stout and faithful and bears about him the marks of loyalty', whilst a little later Margaret Luscombe was described as a person 'held by us to be a fit and able woman for the teaching of little children their ABC and vowels'. Here, then, we have the first school, with its master and dame. The teachers were paid entirely through fees, and it is reasonable to assume that not every child in Brent attended the school. In 1721 James Gibbons was licensed to teach the three Rs, as was Humphrey Marshall in 1746. It was at about this time that John Wilcocks, vicar of Brent between 1672 and 1716, left £100 in his will, dated 1733, to be invested in land for educational purposes. Thomas Acland, vicar between 1716 and 1737, left further money to be laid down in land and in interest for teaching the boys of the town, and of the village of Aish, the basic requirements of literacy. Another endowment amounting to £1 per annum was left by the Revd Robert Bradford in 1800 to buy Bibles for four poor children.

By 1820 we find a dame-school of about 40 children and another 'private' fee-paying school for those who could afford it.

The Belfry

In 1735 Charles Taylor became vicar of South Brent and was succeeded in 1739 by Henry Bradford. William White describes St Petroc's Church, which he mistakenly dedicates to St Patrick, as 'a large ancient fabric, in the decorated style, with a low tower and six bells'. These bells were cast in 1755 during the

Prizewinning bell-ringers from St Petroc's tower. Left to right: *John Eales, Pat Johnstone, Des Sparkes, Charlie Hard, Ray Mugridge and Fernley Rogers.*

(EALES COLLECTION)

St Petroc's bell-ringing team. The picture features: *Sandra Southern, Fernley Rogers, Sally Fox, John Eales, Ken Fox, Suzanne Mugridge, Desmond Sparkes, Julie Sparkes, Charlie Hard, 'Uncle John' Furneaux, George Whiddon, Ray Mugridge, Jim Goss, Angela Valance, Pat Johnstone, ?, Julia Stevens, Linda Rogers and Simon Fox.* (VALLANCE COLLECTION)

incumbency of Walter Taylor, who became vicar in 1744. They are inscribed:

I   *To call Christ's flock, Loud do I ring.*
II   *Success to British Arms.*
III *Fear God and honour the King.*
IV   *Thomas Bilby, Collumpton, cast us all, 1755.*
V   *Walter Taylor, Vicar: J. Hannaford, Richard Veale, Churchwardens.*
VI   *Religion, Death and Pleasure cause me to ring.*

In 1765 John Nosworthy was instituted as vicar of the parish in succession to Walter Taylor.

South Brent has always had a fine body of bell-ringers, who still maintain the old custom of electing their lord chief and crier at an annual meeting. The signatures of all the ringers are then entered in the Ringers' Book. In addition to the names of every ringer since 1778, when John Amyatt was vicar, the book also records the articles and rules of the teams. The original book was replaced for the first time only in 2003, for fear that it might be damaged if used any longer.

The Ringing Society was 'begun the day of 4th Nov Anno Domini 1787', when Henry Manning was the chief speaker, and 12 articles for 'the good intent of the Ringing Society' were laid down. The society would exist as long as there were six members – one for each bell in the tower.

The ringers would elect their lord chief and crier

at an annual dinner to be held on 4 November each year. The articles provided for substantial fines or even exclusion from the society if ringers did not behave in a 'seemly' manner. The fourth article reads:

That if any Ringers Curse, Swear or Prophane the Lord's Almighty name in vain, Promote Gaming or Debauched Discourse in the Society Room at any meeting of the Ringers he shall pay two pence for such Offence or be excluded.

The fifth is equally severe:

If any Ringer at any time of Meeting abuse either the Lord Chief Speaker or the cryer or any other Ringer he shall pay three pence for every such offence and if any Ringer shall strike another at any time of meeting he shall pay six pence for the First Offence one shilling for the Second and be excluded for the Third and no such Excluded Ringer shall ever be admitted again into this Society.

Ringers were also subject to a fine if, unless they were ill, they did not ring when requested to do so. The only members exempt from fines were those over 60 years of age who had been members of the society for 20 years or more. The articles were evidently enforced – on 29 May 1785 one ringer is noted as being excluded from the society.

Mrs Hingston, a village resident and stalwart of the Methodist Church, is presented with a bouquet by Mrs French to celebrate her 90th birthday, 1974.

(Honeywell Collection)

Mrs Pam Honeywell, Mrs Robjohns and Mrs Hawes outside the Methodist Church in the early 1990s.

(Honeywell Collection)

The exterior of the Methodist Church.

South Brent has a reputation for holding flower festivals in all three churches simultaneously. Shown here is a display in the Methodist Church on the theme of Russia in 2000.

Nonconformity Arrives

Whilst researching the origins of Methodism in South Brent for the centenary of the reconstruction of the Methodist Church, Mr Bert Dyer traced the movement back to when a few friends and neighbours met in each other's homes for worship. As numbers quickly grew, so the need for premises larger than someone's front room became necessary. In 1757 an Ugborough miller leased to these early Methodists a store, or barn, at the bottom of Church Street which was converted into the first chapel. In 1813 the miller, by then quite elderly, conveyed the chapel to a body of trustees for a nominal 10s. This is Chapel Cottage, behind No. 1 The Exchange.

The building, although now a church, was still, however, only a converted barn, and by 1812 the Methodists had moved their church to its permanent site on the north side of the street. At the time it stood behind a row of artisans' cottages and was entered through an archway similar to several along the length of the street.

The Methodists were not the only Nonconformist congregation in South Brent. On 20 May 1823, a new independent chapel was opened in Totnes Road, where three sermons were preached by the Revd Messrs Hartly of Plymouth, Windeatt of Totnes and Davis of Kingsbridge. The establishment of the chapel was made possible by a 'pious' lady from Ashburton, who gave £900 to trustees, the interest on which was to be used for the support of an independent minister, who was to reside at South Brent. The Revd W. Sherman, of Newport Pagnell, commenced his ministry in the village, and it was his success which led to the building of the chapel, the lady having stipulated that none of her money

The 1981 St George's Day church parade outside the Methodist Church. The adult leaders are Patsy Tidball, Don Stansbury, Irene McNevin, Adrian Sharville and Adrian Woodhouse. (TIDBALL COLLECTION)

should be used for the provision of a building. The public appeal that was launched did not raise more than £200.

Turnpike Trusts and the End of an Era

Travellers in the area in the seventeenth and eighteen centuries would have taken roughly the same route through Brent as those in former years. The Pack Horse was the main posting house in the village and both coaches and independent travellers would have been able to change horses in a livery stable boasting its own forge. The Pack Horse itself belonged to the Petre family, and rents were taken from Lady Day to Lady Day. At the beginning of the eighteenth century the landlord of the Pack Horse was William Thompson. His annual rent was set at £15, although each year disbursements for the rates, taxes and repairs, plus 9s. for one year's quit rent sunk on the premises, were deducted, bringing his payment to just over £13 per year for the tenancy.

By the mid-eighteenth century, with a greater volume of traffic on the roads, there was a need for a more efficient system of maintenance, and so the Turnpike Trusts were set up. The road from medieval Brent Bridge eastwards came under the control of the Ashburton Turnpike Trust, the fourth such trust to be set up in Devon in 1755.

In operation until 1878, the old toll-house still stands beside the road at Brent Mill. Westwards from Brent Bridge the road was under the control of the Plymouth Eastern Trust and ran past Glazebrook, on through Cheston to Bittaford and thence to Plymouth. It was probably the Ashburton Trust which straightened the route and built a new stretch of road between Yonder Cross and Beara. The Turnpike Trust placed milestones along the roadside, with toll-gates and toll-houses at intervals. It was not until 1834 that the Ashburton Turnpike Trust constructed the 'new' route from Lower Dean to Brent Bridge via Marley, Stidston and Palston.

This is the route that would have been used by the famous Quicksilver Mail, the fastest coach in England, described as 'simply perfection', which had the motto *Nemo me impune lacessit* ('No-one holds me up with impunity'). The Plymouth to London journey took from 8.30p.m. until 4p.m. the next evening at an average 11 miles per hour, with 45 seconds allowed for changing four horses. The first stage, from Plymouth to Ashburton, was driven by one coachman who then waited in Ashburton to bring the down coach back to Plymouth.

During the next 100 years, the face of South Brent probably did not alter a great deal. Unfortunately the Land Tax assessments, which begin in 1745, only mention 'tenements in Town' and give no details of which buildings were owned and/or occupied by those taxed. The Petre survey of 1788 does not reveal any great alterations to the face of Brent and it must be the case that the joining of Brent and Brent Mill and the expansion along Totnes Road (once Barrack Street, so called for the militia barracks at its town end, the outside wall of which remains) and Hillside date from the late-nineteenth and early-twentieth centuries.

The toll-house at Brent Mill, with the old turnpike road going off towards Glazebrook and then on to Bittaford and Ivybridge.

Brent's Characters

Frank Rogers, known as 'Fakum' was one of the village's personalities of the 1950s. He lived in Wellington Square and was known locally as a 'professional mourner' – he never missed a funeral! This picture is also interesting in that it shows Brent's second fish and chip shop at No. 1 The Exchange, which was run by the Huxtables.

(FRED BURROWS COLLECTION)

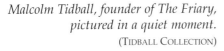

Malcolm Tidball, founder of The Friary, pictured in a quiet moment.

(TIDBALL COLLECTION)

Walter Stumbles Crispin – telegraph boy in South Brent, c.1912. (FRED BURROWS COLLECTION)

Mr Peter Miller at work in the summer of 2000, keeping Brent clean and tidy. Pete took on this job when he became the first person to leave the Slumberland Mill when it closed down.

(MILLER COLLECTION, TAKEN BY DAVID CARROLL)

Two views of Soper's Garage. At one time Brent could boast two garages, Chenhall's and Sopers of South Brent, whose blue stickers could be seen in the backs of many cars in the area. This shows Sopers branch at Manor Garage. Regulations about the distance between petrol pumps and dwellings meant that the Esso franchise was removed, although the sign pole can still be seen. At one stage Sopers, which started in a corrugated-iron building at the end of Palstone Lane, had three outlets in South Brent: Manor Garage, Brooklands and Marley Head Service Station.

The corner of Chapelfields c.1985, before the construction of the new school.

In 1704 the Petre family, as lords of the manor, received an income of £119.1s.¾d., as recorded by John Knight. In 1705 the sum from their Brent lands was £114.9s.10¾d. Out of this total came a donation of £1 to the poor, the cost of homage and jurors' dinners and the salary due to John Knight for collecting the rents. In 1720 John Penhay, the bailiff and rent collector employed by William Shirwill, took possession of land called Wontons on the death of one Jonathan Trist. When Penhay failed to report the death to the steward, pretending that Trist was still alive, new leases were issued. In 1731 he left the lands to his wife, and it was not until 1732 that the fraud came to light.

The end to the Petre era came on 28 April 1826, when John Elliot of Churston, with financial support from William Evens of Plympton (who advanced £7,000) and Richard Derry of Plymouth (who advanced £3,000) bought the manor from the Petre family for £11,000.

In 1810 George Baker became vicar of South Brent.

Rear Admiral (Blue) William Cuming

To the left-hand side of the organ in St Petroc's Church is a memorial by Kendall of Exeter depicting a mourning lady. This memorial is to another of Brent's worthies, Rear Admiral William Cuming.

Rear Admiral Cuming was one of Nelson's commanders at the battle of Copenhagen in 1801, and was in charge of HMS *Russell*, a 74-gun ship of the line. Navigation in the area of the battle was so intricate that the *Russell* was one of two ships to go aground, although, according to the reports, 'was so placed as to be of great service'. The *Russell* lost five seamen and one marine in the battle. William Cuming started his career as a lieutenant on 7 December 1779 and by 28 December 1795 had achieved the rank of commander. During this period of his career, in 1797, he briefly commanded HMS *Victory*, after which he became a captain. Awarded the CB in 1815, he became Rear Admiral on 19 July 1821. Cuming died on 20 June 1824, having served in many operations and on many vessels during his long and varied career.

CHAPTER 4

The Elliott Era, 1826–88

And so begins the next era in the development of Brent – a time when the vicar and churchwardens of South Brent received some of their severest criticisms.

St Petroc's – 'Not in a Fit State of Repair'

In 1824 the Archdeacon of Totnes, the famous R.H. Froude of Dartington, commented:

The Archdeacon is sorry to find that more attention has not been paid to his orders, by the Churchwardens of the parish, and that considerable expense must be incurred before the church can be considered in a fit state of repair.

He gave orders to the vicar, Revd George Baker, and his churchwardens, Mr Thuell and Mr Hosking, that:

A trench must be sunk in an effectual manner round the whole of the exterior wall of the fabric, to the depth of the church floor, provided that no injury be done to the foundations and no recently formed graves be disturbed. Any bones that may be displaced must be carefully

re-interred in a shell provided for the purpose. The weeds should be cut and the walks cleaned three or four times a year.

The door of the tower must be neatly cased. The pavement of all the aisles being rough, uneven and decayed must be relaid. Beginning with the north transept and the small north windows next adjoining the chancel, the stonework of all the windows must gradually be restored throughout until the whole be completed in the same fashion and with the same description of materials as is now used for the mullions and heads. Good clear glass should be substituted for that which is nasty. An old door way on the north side may be walled up. The screen should be painted a light stone colour.

The Churchwardens are in like manner to call on the rector to put the whole of the chancel into a complete and substantial state of repair. The pavement must be worked smooth and laid even and with materials of good quality. The stonework of the windows being much dilapidated must be restored according to the directions already given for those in the body of the church.

No burials are to be permitted within six feet of the Church walls. No long seats must be converted into large pews without authority from the Ordinary.

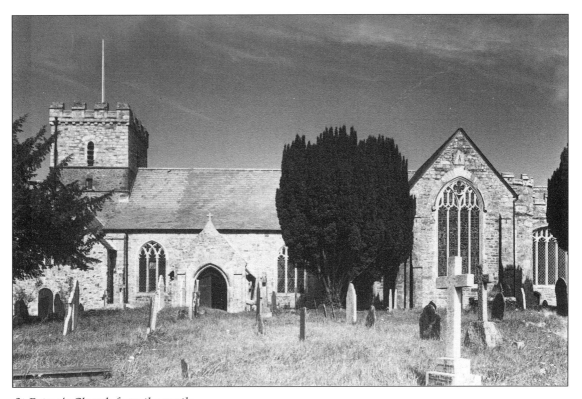

St Petroc's Church from the south.

The Archdeacon expects that a report be made to him in the first week of January next for the progress made in the work.

The best way would be to borrow money under the act for the completion of the whole work at once – but the Churchwardens are left to their own discretion.

Seemingly, however, nothing was done. On 25 April 1825 the rural dean, Revd William Hanley of Stoke Fleming, made his annual visit and made little other comment than that the seats needed to be cleaned and the walls whitewashed. In 1826 another rural dean, Revd R.H. Froude, wrote:

As the Churchwardens have thought proper to pay little attention to orders entered in this book in 1824, it will be my duty to enforce this being carried out with effect by such means as the law affords. The windows throughout the church with exception of that lately repaired by the Vicar and another put in by the Churchwardens on the north side are still in a very bad state of repair – what has been lately done to the stonework of the mullions of the other cannot be considered as a proper sort of repair. I shall also require that all the preceding orders shall be completed with the least possible delay.

By February 1829 the new rural dean, Revd H. Kerr, noted that 'the Churchwardens are proceeding with the repairs of the church but not with the windows'. In 1833 the Revd Richard Stranger drew attention to the poor state of many of the pews and the churchwardens were told 'to use the most effectual means in their power to put a stop to the nuisances which at present disgrace the churchyard' – no mention is made of what the nuisances were. By 23 May 1834 the situation had grown worse and the rural dean gave orders that, 'No thoroughfare is to be allowed through the churchyard'. A new rural dean, Revd R.C. Kitson, found no work had been done and ordered that new bell ropes be procured. By May 1836 still nothing had been done, although in 1839 Revd Joshua Reynolds Johnson gave a slightly better report. Throughout this period mention is made of the need to whitewash the interior walls to cover up damp spots. In 1842 the rural dean finally reported that all was in good condition.

The Coming of the Railway

By the time the railway opened in 1848, much of the original community of Brent was established.

The tithe map of 1842 gives an accurate ground plan of Brent town at that time. It shows a crowded place with the Cheape House dominating the centre. The small courtyards of tiny cottages dominate the length of Church Street, Station Road and Barrack Street, although the corner at the bottom of Church Street curiously seems not yet to have been built on.

An example of these courtyards can still be seen around Nos 26, 27 and 28 Church Street, with another just below the toll-house, known as 'Sunnyside'. There were also cottages in front of where the Methodist Church now stands. Victoria Cottage had five two-up, one-down cottages in its front garden, all of which were demolished after the First World War. The buildings which stand on the site of Nos 1–4 The Exchange were destroyed by fire on 25 February 1901. Although the cottages no longer exist, whether as a result of demolition, of being swallowed up in later development or of catastrophe, the numbering system in Church Street still remains, jumping from Nos 1 and 2 to the early teens, twenties and then to No. 52. Returning for a moment to Victoria Cottage, the tithe map shows a long 'walkway' leading up behind it to a small building, presumably where the station yard now stands. This walkway is believed to have been a ropewalk – a long lane in which the ropes used in rigging boats and ships were twisted and woven. This would fit in with the manufacture of sailcloth at Crackhills at the time. The feature survived until the late 1960s, when it was filled in during work on the cottage garden. In 1842 the lane leading down to Millswood by St Dunstan's Church did not exist, access to that area being via the lane next to the church.

In 1841, for the 1,237 souls living in the parish, Brent Fair was the high spot of the town's commercial year. Apart from various markets, all business was conducted through shopkeepers and craftsmen. It was at this time that the first directories for Devon begin to appear – the forerunners of modern business listings. In 1850 William White published the first comprehensive directory of Devon, from which it is possible to glean an idea of what the population of Brent was like in the mid-nineteenth century. The census of 1851, although sometimes diverging from White's account, provides further information, and from both sources we are able to build a fairly good picture of the townspeople.

In 1850, according to White, there were half a dozen shopkeepers in South Brent (the census suggests a few more), including grocers, dairymen (of which there were three), two or three bakers and butchers John Codd and Henry Hingston. There were also wheelwrights John Clancey and William Cole, blacksmiths William Scobell and William Widdicombe, saddler William White, and harness-maker Thomas Hard – trades vital in a time when the horse was an indispensable part of life. Two thatchers were also listed as working in Brent.

Amongst other tradesmen mentioned are carpenters John Dodd, Nicholas and Richard Heath and Jarvis Veale, plumbers John R. Cranch and William Stidston, masons Peter Ford, Thomas and William Knott and Richard Peathyjohns at Aish, and various painters, all working on the upkeep of Brent's buildings. More personal needs were served by tailors

The view looking down Station Road at the time of the Hospital Week celebrations in 1913. Lily and Eliza Pannell are seen on the right with Mr Blanchard. The entrance to Catt's Garage is on the right of the picture.

(ANDERSON COLLECTION)

Solomon Cole, William Hurrell, Hercules Joynt and William Toope, while there was an even greater number of dressmakers. There were at least six shoemakers, Philip and William Blight, John Eales, Richard Farleigh, John Soper and Henry Veale, and for the ladies a milliner, Miss Turner. One John Lee is listed as a worsted spinner and John Horswell as a woolcomber. Others, not specifically tradesmen, earning a living in the town, included Dr John Mowatt, a surgeon-cum-dentist from Gloucester. Thomas Daykin of Kerswell was also a surgeon, while at the other end of the nineteenth-century social scale were three washerwomen.

The vast majority of those listed in the 1850 direc-

This 1950s view of Station Road shows the stables to the Royal Oak Hotel on the left. (VERA JORDAN COLLECTION)

Royal Oak Cottages showing the original level of the road to the left of the railings. The higher level was created with the coming of the railway.   (MILLER COLLECTION)

tory, however, are males, and are described as farmers. Of the 47 named, ten are referred to as owners. There were also the men who worked and managed the slate quarries for Webber & Co., and those who ran the five taverns in the town – Mr William Ward at the Globe, Mr William Davis at the Pack Horse, Mr William Maunder at the Royal Oak, Mr Arthur Langworthy at the Anchor and, at Brent Mill, Mr George Luscombe at the London Inn. The Globe, which was once opposite the Pack Horse

where Fore Street becomes Totnes Road, has since disappeared. There was possibly a further tavern, the Wheatsheaf, although it is not mentioned in the directory.

Mr R. Mitchell ran the Post Office, from which letters went via Ivybridge. Interestingly, there was a penny post from Ashburton to Brent, and Edward Andrews was the carrier to Plymouth on Saturdays. In the directory Mr John Elliott, lord of the manor, is one of the gentlemen listed as living in Brent, as is

Winzer's butcher's shop, Station Road, in the late-nineteenth century. In 2005 the shop houses a video rental business.   (MEAD COLLECTION)

The Anchor Hotel and Church Street, probably on a sunny Wednesday in the 1950s. Wednesday is early-closing day, which accounts for the lack of traffic.

Winzer's butcher's shop showing Mr Winzer at the door. Note that the shop windows have been removed.

(MEAD COLLECTION)

Captain Augustus Kuper. Augustus Leopold Kuper went on to achieve great things, later becoming an admiral and living at The Rock on the Aune. Kuper Island, off the west coast of Canada, was named after him and nearby Thetis Island after his ship, HMS *Thetis*, the 36-gun frigate in which he surveyed the islands in 1851. During the Opium Wars, in command of HMS *Alligator*, Kuper maintained the blockade of Amoy, in China, and destroyed several war junks, while his failed attempt at forcing a passage between Kolangso and Amoy harbour led the Chinese to believe they had won an important victory.

The Revd Nathaniel Cole had been vicar of Brent since 1845, and his family would remain in the incumbency until 1905. His vicarage is described as 'a good residence near the church'. Revd Gubbins was the independent minister, while no mention is made of a Wesleyan minster, although there was the chapel in Church Street.

The South Devon Railway opened its track past Brent in 1848. The only station between Totnes and Laira Green at that time was Wrangaton, which was a transit point into the South Hams. Wrangaton used to be called Kingsbridge Road – the inn above Wrangaton Station, now the Coach House, was known as the Kingsbridge Road Hotel for many years. The original road changed following the construction of the A38 dual carriageway in the early 1970s. The exact date of the opening of Brent Station is not known, but it was certainly operational by 1849 and in 1850 had a stationmaster, Richard Veale, and two porters to work it, with trains six times a day to Exeter and Plymouth.

(CRANCH COLLECTION)

The cottages at Brent Mill, c.1907. The building on the left was the original London Inn, now known as Clarence House.

Plymouth Road in 2005. No. 1 Plymouth Road is the Pack Horse.

The Royal Oak Hotel, taken before the building of the shop premises at Nos 1 and 1a Station Road.

(MOULDING/NOBLE COLLECTION)

The naphtha works at Shipley Bridge, c.1900. The chimney was demolished by Mr A.W Cranch when it became unsafe.

(Cranch Collection)

The railway track, after it leaves Marley Tunnel in Rattery parish, runs into the north of Brent village, arriving from the east via a cutting, then continues straight through the station, over the River Avon and on towards Plymouth. The line forms what could be described as a 'butcher's hook' as it winds its way through Brent.

When Isambard Kingdom Brunel first worked out the route for the railway through this area in the mid-1830s, he saw it not as skirting the edge of the moor, but rather following a route through the South Hams via Kingsbridge, Modbury and Yealmpton and thence into Plymouth. Luckily for Brent, that route did not materialise.

The original single-track line was widened when the Great Western Railway took over following the merger of the Bristol & Exeter, the South Devon Railway and the Great Western Railway in February 1876.

Although there is no record of what the original Brent Station looked like, it would appear that in the early 1860s the station moved from the south side of the line to the north side. The main building was of chalet style and constructed in wood. The signal-box, a Saxby 8 Farmer type 4 design, comes from a later period, and is thought to have opened in around November 1875.

Industrial Beginnings

The mid-nineteenth century saw attempts to exploit some of the natural resources on Brent Moor. The ruins at Shipley Bridge are of the naphtha works which once flourished there, opened by Messrs Davy & Wilkin of Totnes. Naphtha, an inflammable oil derived from the distillation of peat, was used for making gas and candles. On 11 June 1846 L.H. Davy and William Wilkin leased land at Redlake from the Duke of Cornwall with the right to 'cut, manufacture and sell peat and peat charcoal'. The lease is kept in the Devon Record Office. In 1847 they built the four-mile long Zeal Tor, or Redlake, tramway, whose 5ft gauge wooden rails were bolted to granite blocks, with horses used to draw the small wooden trucks along the track. However, this project did not last long and the partnership was dissolved in 1850, with Davy and Wilkins allowed to carry on 'certain works called the Ashburton Gas Works' whilst the company was wound up.

In 1855 Gerald and Francis Meynell of Brent Moor

Oakhill corner showing the junction between the Lutton hill and the road to Lydia Bridge. The large house on the right is Oakhill. At the bottom of the hill is The Rock on the Aune. (CRANCH COLLECTION)

The London Inn at Brent Mill, 2005.

House granted Mr William Saunders a lease to extract china clay from Brent Moor. The Meynells, however, kept the right to the Zeal Tor tramway. Mr Saunders then sold the lease to the Brent Moor China Clay & Mica Work Co. Ltd in 1858. Mr Saunders himself gained permission from the Duchy to cut a leat to the settling pits at Shipley. After the Duchy had negotiated a substantial rent the leat was completed and in use by the middle of 1859. On the same site two men, Hall and Hill, started the South Brent China Clay Co. in 1872. Unfortunately, the china clay was of a poor quality, making production costs too high, and in 1876 the company is recorded as being in 'financial difficulties to such an extent that they could not pay the rent for the leat.' The clay was extracted at Petre's Pits and brought down the old naphtha tramway to be processed at the Shipley Bridge end. One of these pits is known as Hall's Pit, the other as Hill's Pit. The micas, or settling pits, can still be seen, all of them connected together at lower levels. This was the last attempt to industrialise Brent Moor.

The first documentary evidence of quarrying and mining appears in the survey book of Robert Withall, dated about 1580. He mentions that:

... there is divers places in this manner quarreys of slate stones which for the most part the tennents save for the coverings of their houses.

He also complains of the way in which other stones are taken for use as millstones and by the masons of the village for illicit trading. There is mention of tinning on Brent Moor in the same document, although it is noted that most of the valuable metal has already been taken. Peat, or moor-coal, was also taken from the moor in great quantities, and there was iron, thought to be of good quality, in the vicinity of Brent Hill.

Nearer to the town was Webber's Quarry at Oakhill. The road that runs to Aish along by the vicarage is still known to some as Quarry Road.

St Petroc's – a Disgrace to the Church People of the Parish

By the mid-nineteenth century concerns were being raised again about the state of the 'large ancient fabric' of St Petroc's Church. The plaster ceiling became decayed and in 1847 the rural dean noted that the woodwork at the base of the screen was also quite rotten, a fact confirmed in the same year in his 'Church Notes' by R. Davidson, who agrees that parts of the screen were badly in need of repair. The rural dean continues, 'but with so noble a church it appears a pity that some little effort be made to keep it in a state becoming the House of GOD.'

In 1848 the then vicar of Brent and rural dean, Revd Nathaniel Cole, concerned himself with the rotting seats under the singing gallery, which stretched across the west end of the nave. Successive rural deans had increasingly severe comments to make: that the ceiling was falling down due to the decay of laths and plaster, especially over the pulpit;

that slates were being used to replace broken glass in the windows and, despite it being noted in 1859 that, 'A new organ has been erected and the gallery lowered to receive it which has greatly improved the general appearance of the church,' in 1860 Revd Hare wrote:

There is much in this church which requires restoration and improvement and it is understood that there is an intention of raising means for effecting these desirable objects.

In 1861 a full report on the state of the church, produced by Mr J. Hine, declared that the roof was 'absolutely dangerous'. The committee for church repairs commissioned him to draw up plans and estimates for the thorough repair of the church which, it was hoped, would be completed by the following year. Such was the state of repair on 4 April 1864 that Revd R. Champernowne, rural dean, wrote, 'The Church, which ought to be one of the finest in the deanery, appears to have been one of the most neglected.'

On 15 March 1865 he further comments, 'The Church is in the same disgraceful state as heretofore.'

In 1866 William Speare Cole became vicar of South Brent, but by all accounts nothing was done, for on 25 April 1870 Mr Champernowne makes his most scathing comment:

It is useless to say anything about the Church, except that it is in the same wretched condition as it has been for many years and is gradually getting worse. It is a disgrace to the 'Church people' in the parish.

A severe criticism indeed of the authorities.

By the time of its restoration in 1870, therefore, St Petroc's Church was in a terrible state of repair. Ironically, it is perhaps fortunate that the church was not renewed in 1862, as there was then a possibility of it being demolished and totally rebuilt, as so many churches were at that time, thus losing any features of architectural interest. As it was, when it was finally restored, or rather restructured, in 1870, the building was to be radically altered in appearance.

Probably the greatest change to take place inside the church was the removal of the rood-screen and reredos, which were very large and highly painted. Revd S. Baring-Gould of Lewtrenchard wrote of such screens:

So rich and elaborate are these latter, that when a church has to be restored, the incumbent trembles at the prospect of renovating his screen, and this has led to many of them being turned out and destroyed. South Brent was thus wantonly destroyed and allowed to rot.

We do, however, have a description (gathered from various sources) of what the church was like. One or two fragments have been replaced, including the First World War memorial table, the main altar rails, the main beam of the belfry screen, and the decoration in the Catherine Chapel. Revd Baring-Gould describes the rood-screen as large and highly decorated, having tracery similar to that at Ugborough, with crockets and spandrels. The church gallery', was stated as being of the worst possible description'. Each aisle had three bays and there were five in the nave, one presumably a door or gate. The design of the carving was similar to that on the present pulpit and there were heraldic devices carved on the panels, one of which bore the arms of the Petre family, the

There has been a butcher's shop at the lower end of Church Street for many years. When this photograph was taken, in the late-nineteenth century, it belonged to Mr William Goodman, seen here in the doorway of his shop with his men around him.

first secular lords of the manor of Brent. From these descriptions, and from the remains which are now restored to the church, the screen and similar reredos must have been magnificent.

Behind the altar, the reredos had seats placed against it, and the plugs which held the structure to the east wall of the chancel can still be seen. This must have resulted in the altar being placed quite a long way out into the chancel. When the wooden structure was removed, a curtain was placed along the whole length of the wall. This has, in its turn, been replaced.

Although all the windows were replaced in the drastic restoration of 1870, the records of Davidson (1847) tell us that the replacements were very similar in design to the originals. There are Early English, Perpendicular and Decorated windows, with the addition of one or two lancets. The Perpendicular are made up of three or four lights with cinquefoil heads, while the Early English have three trefoil lights with intersecting tracery.

. . . and in 1870

Many of the tradesmen who appeared in the 1850 directory were still trading in 1870. William Scoble was still working as a blacksmith and had been

A carnival street fair. Hobbs Bros were butchers who took over the business on Mr Jeff White's retirement.

joined by George Ball and Henry Clancy, who is also described as a wheelwright. Both Philip Blight and John Farleigh were still trading as shoemakers and had been joined by Richard Leaven junr. Jarvis Veale had by then become the deputy parish clerk and Mr Fred Parr had taken over as stationmaster. Mr Henry Veale had become postmaster, and at the same time was trading as a shoemaker. Interestingly, two of the publicans appear to have to worked in other trades – William Davis of the Pack Horse is also described as a market-gardener and James Hosking of the Globe as a tailor. William Ward had moved from the Globe to the London Inn and William Petherbridge had taken over the Royal Oak. What seems remarkable about the 1870 listings is the number of people described as running apartments and lodging houses – seven of them in all.

Once again, however, it is in farming that we find that greatest number of people employed. Such names as Savery, Goodman, Wakeham, Codd and Andrews feature in the 1870 list of farmers, just as they do in the modern *Yellow Pages*.

In the 1860s Messrs Peter Adams & Co. used the mills at Millswood for the manufacture of paper. When the paper-mill failed the premises were for some years used to produce flock and shoddy, and then in the making of compressed leather, an enterprise which also failed. Thomas Richards was the manager of the Brent Mill factory, while John Helmore is described as a miller. It is at this trade that one of Brent's more famous inhabitants tried his hand.

William Crossing

The mill at Crackhills, which began life as a flour mill, later became, under the Crossing family, one of the principal sail-canvas mills for the Devon ship-building industry. Thus South Brent can lay claim to well-known author William Crossing, whose father co-owned the mill with Mr J.H. Philp. Older Brentonians, in 2005, can still remember 'Billy Crossing'. Indeed it is during his time in Brent that he began to take an interest in Dartmoor, on which subject he is posthumously acknowledged as an authority.

William moved to Island House after his marriage to Emma Witheridge of Ivybridge in 1872, and was employed to manage the mill when Mr Philp left to pursue other interests. William and Emma then moved to Splatton. William had two great passions – the theatre and the moor. He even formed his own theatrical company, which he took on tour. By the mid-1870s the mill was in financial straits and was repossessed by the bank. When William persuaded them to reduce the rent, the business struggled on. In 1874 William began to keep records of Dartmoor, and his books *Crosses*, *Tales of the Dartmoor Pixies* and *Amid Devonia's Alps* were all published while he lived

The South Brent butcher's shop, in 2005 run by Neil Langworthy.

in Brent. By 1880, with 29 people employed at the mill, the tide seemed to have turned. William's great passions, however, kept him from his work at the mill, and with the advent of steam power the business collapsed financially.

Crackhills Mill now stands as a gaunt ruin next to the path to the weir. From this same weir, beside which the mill's two sluices can still be seen, ran the leat which powered the mill, setting in motion the iron mill-wheel before flowing back into the river.

William Crossing became a coal merchant and in 1897 he and Emma moved to West Devon, where he died in 1928 and was buried in Mary Tavy churchyard.

St Petroc's – a Pleasure to Inspect

The church having been 'restored' in 1870, no further entries were made in the rural dean's log until 1877, when Revd R. Bartholomew wrote, 'I am happy in being able to give a very different report from my predecessor on the other page.'

In 1882 Revd J.B. Hughes commented that 'South Brent church was a pleasure to inspect.' Three years later he wrote, 'There is not a slate mounting out of place or a pane of glass broken.'

In 1887 the vicar and churchwardens were congratulated on the introduction of a surpliced choir.

The 1890s saw concern being expressed about the bearings of the bells and the timbers of the ringing loft, so in 1894 the bells were rehung by Mr Stokes of Woodbury for £107 and the building was insured for £3,000. The same decade saw various gifts presented to the church culminating, on Friday 15 April 1898, in a new and grander organ being dedicated by the Archdeacon of Totnes.

In 1901 Revd Charles Martin wrote of St Petroc's, in words the very opposite of those written by Mr Champernowne 37 years earlier, that, 'The Church is one of the most beautiful in the deanery and is in excellent order.'

The comments of the rural deans reveal other interesting facts. There was at one time a ceiling of plaster in the building and a bell-ringers' gallery. We also know that the screen, pews and communion rails were all painted, and that the walls, although whitewashed to cover up the damp spots, were not themselves plastered. The ringing loft cannot have been taken out until the end of the nineteenth century, as it is mentioned as being unsafe in 1891. Again, despite talk of putting a screen across the belfry as early as 1903, this, in 2005, has only recently been done.

An interesting reference, found in an account of a visit to Brent by Dean Jeremiah Milles, suggests that in the eighteenth century the tower may well have sported a spire and pinnacles. Milles maintains that there were then five bells, whereas now there are six.

Moving through the nineteenth century, the population of Brent remains stable. In 1861 there were 1,205 souls living in Brent, which is mentioned as a polling-place for the south division of the county, its district comprising Brent, Buckfastleigh, Dean-Prior, Diptford, Halwell, Holne, Ivy Bridge, Modbury, Morley, North Huish, Totnes and Ugborough.

The Birth of the Board School

The directory of 1850 mentions Miss Sophia Hosking as a schoolmistress, presumably of the free school, with land endowed by Revd Wilcocks and Revd Acland. It appears, however, that this did not develop into a church school, as happened in many other places.

Under the provisions of the 1870 Education Act, parishes in which there was no 'voluntary' school were required to set up a board and maintain a school financed from the parish rates. As there was no church school in Brent a school board was established in 1874. With no existing building, one was constructed at a cost of £2,080, the board having borrowed a total of £2,500 from the Public Works loan department.

With the building completed in the latter part of 1876 the board determined the regulations. The pupils were to spend five hours a day, five days a week in school, and were to have six weeks' holiday during the year. In those days parents had to pay for the education of their children, and in 1876 South Brent Board School fees were set at:

Age	labourers	others
Under 7s	1d.	4d.
7–10	2d.	6d.
11–13	3d.	8d.
14+	1s.reduced to 8d. if passing inspection	

The board also determined that religious instruction should be Bible-based but non-denominational.

The mill at Crackhills, once owned by William Crossing's family, from an oil painting by A.L. Mitchell.

The canvas mill at Crackhill, once run by William Crossing. In the background is Webber's Quarry.

(CRANCH COLLECTION)

The weir above Crackhills Mill. This weir drove the water-wheel which in turn drove the mill machinery.

(CRANCH COLLECTION)

In January 1877 Mr Samuel Price, accompanied by his wife Emma, took up his position as the first headmaster of South Brent Board School. His salary was £100 plus half of the grant awarded to the school each year by the government.

Mr Price enrolled 165 children between the ages of 3 and 15½ years in his first week as headmaster, most of whom had no experience of the rigours of school. It is thus not surprising that he comments, 'The Brent Children are under no control, and are as wild and untrained as any. I kept capital order by voice and eye alone.'

The regulations set down by the board meant that he could not resort to corporal punishment. He added later, however, that despite the warning he had been given before arriving in Brent, 'the Brent boys are undoubtedly, a wild and vigorous lot of lads, but they are remarkably well disposed and tractable.'

The first inspection by Her Majesty's Inspectors gave a good report, although Mr Price commented that his inability to use corporal punishment did put a 'very great strain' on him.

The year 1877 was good for whortleberries and local traditions did not die with the advent of the board school – many children went picking the moorland fruit instead of attending school. Mr Price duly noted, 'Whortleberries 6d. a quart: I shall be heartily glad when they are gone.'

Similarly, in 1880 he records that mushrooms were fetching 1d. per lb, hence there were absences.

In 1878 the infants became a separate department under a mistress who was paid £60p.a., easing the burden on Mrs Price. In 1879 Her Majesty's Inspectors, who were not much given to praising the work of schools, reported with rare enthusiasm that:

Few schools deserve more thoroughly than this one to be called excellent in all respects. Discipline and instruction are alike admirable; and the general tone is remarkable for the bright and intelligent interest that the boys show in their work.

In 1880 it was reported that the school 'steadily maintains its excellent character... the South Brent Board Schools present an admirable example of the organisation and working of three Departments.'

When the Prices left in December 1880 their resignation was accepted 'with regret'.

At the same time, the question of what to do with

South Brent Board School, which opened in 1874 and served countless young Brentonians until 1997, when it became the Old School Community Centre. Note the bellcote over the front entrance (left), *and the building as it is now* (right).

(NOBLE/MOULDING COLLECTION AND JAMES FORD COLLECTION)

the endowment income of the defunct parish dame-school was at last settled, and the board, after much palaver, persuaded the Charity Commission that the money should be used to pay school fees for the 'deserving poor other than paupers' (the latter having their fees paid by the guardians), and for 'binding and educating blind, deaf and dumb, cripples, etc., to trades.'

Mr and Mrs James Pierce arrived in January 1881. They had difficulty in keeping discipline without the use of corporal punishment, and Mrs Pierce found the girls 'talkative and a little awkward'. The board recognised that use of the cane might be necessary and gave permission for it. Both Mr and Mrs Pierce used it in extreme cases, much to the displeasure of both board and parents. Mr Pierce did not find Brent an easy place to live or work, as his comments show:

The morality of this neighbourhood is of such a debased character that all the good influence received at this school is immediately counterbalanced by it. Lying I have never before met with to such an extent.

Mr Pierce also mentions that, 'Brent children are the dirtiest I have ever met with, as I am compelled to examine each child every morning to see that they come decent.'

In 1882 the fees were changed, presumably in order not to discourage the potential workforce from staying on after Standard 4.

Age	labourers	others
Under 7s	1d.	2d.
7–10	2d.	4d.
11–13	3d.	6d.
13+	4d.	7d.
If passing Standard 4	8d.	10d.

Mr and Mrs Pierce left at midsummer 1883 and went to North Tawton on the other side of the moors, which must have suited them better since they stayed there until 1920, when Mr Pierce retired.

In July 1883 Mr and Mrs Harris took charge of South Brent Board School. He had to use the cane three weeks after arriving, and thence used it severely and freely. In 1884 a gang of louts frightened a group of girls on their way from Avonwick and stole their lunches. The boys were gaoled.

Mr Harris also noted, 'The morals of the parents of this village are anything but good,' but 'I have never met with boys who worked with such good spirit as the lads in this school.'

Mr Harris was rather too over-expectant of the children. He set Standard 1, the seven-year olds, the sum: $192,132,022 \times 9009$, although their standard required not much more than basic arithmetic. In 1889 he set the following exam, to Standard 4:

1. Reduce 3,196 years to seconds.
2. Reduce 10 miles to inches.
3. Difference in pints between 391 hogsheads of beer and 473 tierces of wine.
4. Reduce 391 £s, crowns, half-crowns, shillings, sixpences, pence, halfpence to £.s.d.

His comment was 'very disappointing indeed', although the questions set were to a standard two or three grades higher!

The board was responsible for ensuring the attendance of the children in school. The attendance officer, who was also the postman, was rather inefficient. He never visited the houses of absentees but rather spoke to the parents in the street, to little effect. Once the parents found out that prosecution was not likely to follow non-attendance it became inevitable that they would take no notice of the attendance officer. The fact that some board members were themselves employing the schoolchildren did not help. Mr Harris began to send out letters himself, but with little effect. Unfortunately for the staff their salaries were dependent on regular attendance and when attendance was poor it was necessary to repeat lessons constantly to ensure good results at the annual inspection.

CHAPTER 5

The Kingwell Era, 1888–1927

The bottom of Church Street, c.1913, with Dick Hard, son of J.S. Hard, with one of his father's horses on the way to Lydia Bridge to pick up a cart. The sign outside the building at the end of the terrace on the right-hand side shows the position of the original Police Station. (INEZ JORDAN COLLECTION)

The School

Mr Caleb Harris and his wife Elizabeth came to South Brent in 1883. Relations between members of the school board and the Harrises were not always easy, and this was particularly the case with Mr J.R.T. Kingwell, the lord of the manor. In 1888 there was an angry altercation over punishment, resulting in a minute-book entry which stated that the board regretted 'his conduct before the Board and fear that if he cannot keep his temper in school better than he did at the Board meeting, it is very bad for the conduct of the school.'

In 1889 the board complained that, 'many entries in the logbook are such as should not be entered' – no doubt including his frequent criticisms of illegal employment of the pupils by board members – and in 1890 (after an election had returned the vicar, three farmers, and a publican) Mr Kingwell made public allegations against Mr Harris, who vehemently refuted them in the local Press. Mr Kingwell then

tried to have Mr Harris censured for defending himself. By a casting vote, however, an amendment was carried that: 'the Schoolmaster [was] perfectly justified in replying to the charges brought against him, such charges if not answered being calculated to damage his reputation.'

Mr Kingwell then attempted to get Mr and Mrs Harris dismissed, but this too failed to get any support.

In 1886 the vicar had arranged for the introduction of a diocesan inspector and a church catechism, but two years later the latter was pronounced illegal and withdrawn. Late in 1894 a prolonged struggle ended with rejection of the diocesan inspection and syllabus, and an invitation to the vicar and the Nonconformist minister to inspect jointly on a 'Bible read and explained' basis. The vicar, Revd William Speare-Cole, refused to co-operate. The board accepted a syllabus drawn up by Mr Harris, and invited joint diocesan and Nonconformist inspection: the diocese refused and so the minister was elected a

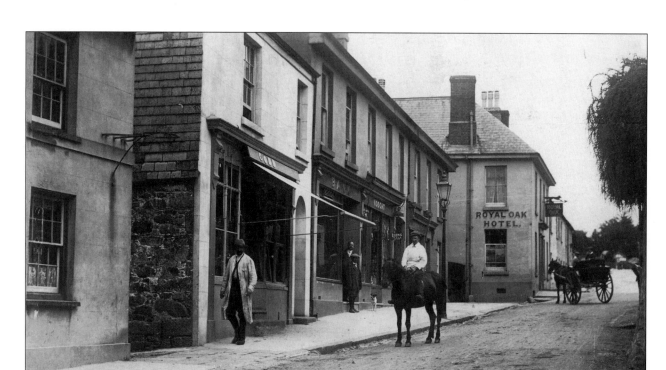

A view of Station Road at the turn of the twentieth century, one of the W.R. Gay series of photographs. The man on the horse is Mr Frank Newman, Margaret Eales's father. (EALES AND CRANCH COLLECTIONS)

member of the board and inspected on his own.

The Harrises are remembered for their 'treats' – tea parties with entertainment. This initiative, designed to bring the school into contact with parents and the community, became an annual event in the life of the school.

South Brent Board School was progressive in that corporal punishment was used only in 'aggravated' cases and then only by the headmaster.

Between 1878 and 1906 the boys and older girls were separated from the infants and younger girls, but in 1906 the school reorganised as a mixed junior and infant school. At one time there were 105 boys on the school register. At first the only assistants were pupil-teachers and monitors, the board finding it too expensive to engage certified assistants. Those who were employed, however, were generously paid – in 1884 Frank Palmer, once a pupil-teacher, was paid £52, but was sacked in an economy drive. He eventually became headmaster at Loddiswell. In

This view of Station Road, although taken 100 years ago, is easily recognisable today. Mr Frank Newman is shown on his horse outside Winzer's, one of the Brent butchers. Only the bank remains on the same site. (MEAD COLLECTION)

The top of Plymouth Road before the First World War. The photograph shows Mrs Elizabeth Hard and Mr Kitson, the landlord of the Pack Horse, outside the hostelry. Milly, Gladys and Jimmy Rowlands are seated on the steps of their cottage with their mother. On 25 January 1912 the Pack Horse was sold to Mr W.J. Goodman for £1,575. It had previously been bought by the Devon Public House Co. in 1903 for £2,800, but even though parts had been sold off it still made a loss of £975.

1893 Frank Sanders was paid £35 and Frank Mumford £55, but in 1894 the board had another economy drive. In the same year C.V. Bidmead was appointed at a salary of £50. Economy drives were common at Brent Board School and Mr and Mrs Pierce left rather than accept a £10 cut in wages. In 1884, however, Mr and Mrs Harris were given an extra £10, which was duly taken away again in 1886. In 1890 the grant was cut by £8.11s.3d., which, needless to say, was deducted from the Harrises' salary.

Acquire any Improvement in this Place!

After further confrontation, especially with Mr Kingwell, who had returned to the board and had taken the chair, the Harrises left for Bristol in 1897. Their pupils gave them a silver matchbox, the parishioners gave a marble clock, and there was a Queen Anne silver tea service from the cricket club.

The next head teacher of Brent School was Mr Wyndham Hull. He took up his post in June 1897 and remained until his retirement in September 1923, after which time he continued to live in Brent until his death in 1941. When Mr and Mrs Hull arrived they found no timetable, no approved schemes of work, no progress records and no complete register. Mr Hull soon remedied the situation.

He and his wife Martha are reported to have been more easy-going than their predecessors. Their logbooks contain relatively few complaints, less vigorously expressed. Mr Hull mildly observed of the rural Devon tempo soon after his arrival that, 'It takes an extraordinary amount of time to set in

motion and afterwards to acquire any improvement in this place.'

On the eve of county take-over of the running of the school in 1902, grant-share was excluded from salaries and the Mr and Mrs Hull were paid a flat £200p.a. The infants' mistress was then still getting £60, and the assistant staff remuneration, notably better than in Harris's time, was:

	Staff	Salary
Boys	1 uncertified	£51.10s.
	1 uncertified	£30
	1 pupil-teacher	£14
Girls	1 uncertified	£25
	1 supplementary	£14
	1 pupil teacher	£14
	2 monitresses	1s. per week
Infants	1 monitress	£12

The Hulls continued the annual concerts started by Mr and Mrs Harris, and five successive events raised £21 for a new school piano.

Dr Sellman comments that:

For all its shortcomings, there were far worse rural School Boards than that of Brent; and the Board School, in its 27 years of existence brought a civilising influence as well as, for the first time, regular and efficient education open to all local children.

But by the start of the twentieth century, times and ideas had changed.

The 1902 Education Act, which took effect in the autumn of 1903, abolished local school boards and transferred control of Brent Board School to the

51

Edwardian Brent

Fore Street, c.1910, showing the Post Office façade before it was altered. Barclay's Bank was housed in the left-hand side of what is now the Mare and Foal. (ONE OF THE W.R. GAY PHOTOGRAPHS IN THE PANNELL COLLECTION)

A photograph taken at the same time of Fore Street looking towards Totnes Road. (CRANCH COLLECTION)

The centre of South Brent, c.1910, showing the jubilee lamppost in its original position. Behind the Pratt's petrol sign we can see the cottages where the Co-op now stands. At the bottom of Church Street the new buildings Nos 1–4 The Exchange date the picture after 1902 but before 1926. (CRANCH COLLECTION)

The Plymouth gas-makers' outing passes the Pack Horse, 1903. (STEER COLLECTION)

County Education Committee. A new era thus opened which was to see changes, both gradual and, at times, drastic.

The Methodist Church Enlarges

In 1887 the Methodist Church had been significantly reconstructed. Historian Mr Bert Dyer notes that:

It was enlarged, lengthened and a gallery was added; in the process the original foundation stone was removed and a new stone 1887 was inserted in the new front wall of the greatly altered and extended Church.

In the period after the First World War many of the small cottages on Church Street were demolished, including the five in front of the church and those in front of Victoria Cottage next door.

Mr Dyer notes that:

The official Chapel Returns from the circuit in 1863 gave the Pew Seats Accommodation as 80 seats free and 80 let. In Victorian times the Church saw the need of a sure, regular income so they rented out a seat or family pew to an individual for a fee.

Mr Dyer can recall an incident when:

An elderly lady came rather belatedly into Chapel to find her seat taken by a visitor. Turning indignantly on her heels she marched out protesting 'I paid rent and sat in that seat for 40 years and I'll sit in no other'.

It was in 1934 that the Methodist Church adopted an envelope system for its income, by which the collec-tion was donated in pre-dated envelopes.

The Methodist Church is organised into circuits, South Brent originally being part of the unwieldy South Devon mission, which had over 40 chapels, from Widecombe to the south coast and from Broadhempston to South Brent. This was later divided in half and is now reduced to a manageable eight chapels.

Mr Dyer mentions the early tradition of the weekly class meeting led by a class leader who took on pastoral duties. These meetings were visited quarterly and would issue class tickets – a sort of membership card. The class leader would preach on the text printed on the ticket and members would pay their class money, which went directly towards the minister's salary.

South Brent Around 1890 –
'Formerly a Market Town'?

In 1850 William White described South Brent as 'formerly a market town'. From the perspective of 1890 it would appear that Mr White was prema-ture in his description, the late-nineteenth and early-twentieth centuries seeing a resurgence in the commercial and industrial-economic status of the town.

Between 1850 and 1950 Brent had four major fairs or markets each year, one of which, known as the 'lamb fair', was held on the last Tuesday and Wednesday in April. The 'goose fair' was the coun-terpart of the Michaelmas fair but was held on the last Tuesday and Wednesday in September. Both fairs were held 'under the glove', a reference to an old, though by no means unique, custom of hoisting

Tom Folland, a local baker, walking along Station Road. Tom is Margaret Eales's grandfather, and the picture, taken at the turn of the twentieth century, is from her collection.

The toll-house showing the Brent Fair charges in 1889, when J.H. Bunker was the collector.

a stuffed white glove in some prominent position to signify freedom from arrest and permission to sell goods for the duration of the fair. In Brent this was done from the Cheape House, which once stood beside the Anchor Hotel at the top of Church Street. When this building was demolished the custom was continued at the toll-house.

Brent Fair was, of course, the really important commercial event of the year. It was something of a national event, with buyers coming from all over the country. Trading took place in the streets, which were thronged with people selling and buyers looking over the cattle, sheep, ponies and other livestock offered for trade. It was impossible to drive a vehicle through the streets and barricades were erected in front of the cottages along the street to prevent windows and doors being broken. Older villagers still tell tales of runaway animals and the chaos that they caused.

On Brent Fair days the town was more like a colossal farmyard, with sheep sold in Wellington Square and the church car park and the whole area filled with penned animals. Church Street was used for the sale of cattle, while the saddler from Exeter set himself up on the Anchor corner and horses were to be found along Station Road. Gypsies came to buy and sell ponies – the main attraction for 'foreigners'.

A report of about 1904 records that in the three weeks after the Brent Fair 500 ponies were sent to the Welsh collieries.

In 1907 Mr Rowe noted that: 'Brent has the reputation as a centre where Dartmoor Ponies may be bought in the same way as Bampton and its fair is the centre for Exmoor ponies.'

By 1890 other fairs were making an impact. There were three good cattle markets held on the last Tuesdays of August, November and February and, at about the same time, a successful pannier market was held every week, proving so successful that it rivalled and drew trade from the market at Totnes. To give others a chance, it was decided to change the day from Friday to Tuesday.

Saturday was the weekly market-day for other goods, with traders coming from the neighbouring parishes to buy and sell. These markets were held under the Cheape House, business commencing in the middle of the morning and continuing as long as there were goods to buy and sell.

In 1890 William White published another directory which gives us a picture of the town at that time. Brent, although larger, was much the same as it had been in 1850. As well as bakers, builders, and bootmakers we find a registrar of births, deaths and marriages, a coal merchant, a chimney sweep, a china-keeper, a watchmaker, and one or two other occupations not mentioned 40 years earlier, which had emerged with the increase in importance of the town. There are, naturally, some changes. Richard Veale had been succeeded by Frederick Parr at the station, which by this time had come under the control of the Great Western Railway. Although the Globe Inn is not mentioned in the 1890 directory, the Pack Horse was still under the control of William Davis, now aged 77. The Royal Oak was now run by Mr William Petherbridge Arscott, the Anchor by Mr Edwin Wakeham, and the London Inn by Mr Joseph Maunder. The Codd family still ran a butchery and there was still a blacksmith called William Scobell, while Mr Tope still ran a 'reputable' tailoring shop. Many firms were obviously family enterprises handed down from father to son.

The Post Office has been one of the centres of Brent's business life for many years. In 1850 letters had gone out from Mr R. Mitchell's shop via Ivybridge. In 1890 there was a Post, Money Order and Telegraph Office at Mr Henry Veale's. Letters were received at 7.40a.m. and 5.00p.m. on weekdays and at 7.40a.m. on Sundays. They were despatched at 12.05p.m. and 8.15p.m. on weekdays, when they went via Exeter. Money order and savings bank business was done from 8.00a.m. to 6.00p.m. on weekdays and from 8.00a.m. to 8.00p.m. on Saturdays. The telegraph office was open from 8.00a.m. to 8.00p.m. on weekdays and from 8.00 to 10.00a.m. on Sundays. Mail was also collected from Brent Mill at 8.10p.m., but on weekdays only.

Jack Crockrem, auctioneer, with Luscombe Maye selling sheep at the 1954 sheep fair.

Auctioneer Ian Blackler selling sheep at Brent sheep sale. To his right is 'Nutty' Newman, one of Brent's characters. Nutty worked as a deliveryman for W.H. Hawke & Son, the coal and corn merchants, who had their office and yard by Lower Station Bridge. He was not particularly tall and is remembered for sliding the sacks of coal straight onto his shoulder from the lorry. He and Bill Hockaday were also responsible for giving the coal lorry a thorough clean down before it could be used as the carnival queen's float each summer. (LUSCOMBE MAYE COLLECTION)

Brent Fair showing the horse and ponies being sold in Plymouth Road. The photograph was taken between 1900 and 1909. (ANDERSON COLLECTION)

railway, which at the time of writing is a tree-covered ruin beside the railway bridges at the end of the vicarage lawn. Its leat runs through the vicarage fields, regulated by a sluice at the Lydia Bridge end. The wheel which drove it must have been on the vicarage side of the structure, that being the side along which the leat runs.

Hawke moved to Millswood, installing new machinery and equipment. The flour was ground by Mr Goss the miller, the smell of it still fresh in the minds of Brentonians who played as children in the fields below. The building was five storeys high and three employees' cottages stood in the yard below. Realising the need for a large hall to serve the people of Brent at this time (1900), Hawke provided a hall measuring 60ft by 40ft, complete with a stage and electric lighting.

After being used as a flour mill, Millswood was taken over as an engineering works by Messrs W.H. Heath of Plymouth and during the First World War was used to make aeroplane parts. The Heaths remained at the mill until 8 February 1948, when it burned to the ground. David Carroll recalls that there were problems for the fire-fighters because the hoses were not compatible with the hydrants and water had to be taken directly from the river.

The Blizzard of 1891

One of the most famous events of this period was the Great Blizzard of 1891.

On Monday 9 March 1891 the day dawned fine and bright. No-one could have predicted that by the

Millswood mills had fallen out of use when Mr W.H. Hawke bought them at the turn of the last century to use as cider stores. Hawke then decided to abandon the small mill that he rented near the

Brent Fair, September 1908. The ponies, having been sold, are penned by Higher Station Bridge ready to be taken by rail to their new owners. Many ended up in the coal mines of South Wales. (CRANCH COLLECTION)

The bottom of Church Street in the early-twentieth century. The cottages that stood in from of the Methodist Chapel and Victoria Cottage (centre left) *have been demolished.* (CRANCH COLLECTION)

South Brent before the advent of the motor car. (PANNELL COLLECTION)

A nineteenth-century scene in Church Street. John Scott Hard is seen at his front door in the centre of the picture.

(DON STANSBURY COLLECTION)

Frank Newman delivering on horseback outside Codd the butcher's in 1913.　　　(EALES COLLECTION)

evening the whole of the South West of England would be gripped in one of the worst snow-storms within living memory. The whole area, not least Brent, came to a grinding halt. Most famously, Brent temporarily became host to the Zulu express, on its way from London. Snow fell from Monday afternoon until Wednesday morning. It was reported that the depth of snow in the town was so great as to be frequently above the windows and doors of the houses. The Zulu was due into Plymouth at 8.55 on Monday night, but came to grief at Brent Station. Published in 1891, author unknown, *The Blizzard in the West, Being a Record and Story of the Disastrous Storm*, which was based on reports in the *Western Morning News* and the *Western Daily Mercury*, read:

> ... *a number of passengers spent several days of that week in this very bleak locality. Especial discomfort appears to have prevailed here, probably on account of the difficulty of obtaining assistance or information from any neighbouring town, and from the limited resources for personal comfort that the town afforded. There can be no doubt that the experiences of the first two days and nights must have been wretched in the extreme. After two hours waiting in the carriages, in a state of considerable doubt as to what was to happen, the travellers found themselves at length at the Brent station1. Here there was neither refreshment nor accommodation, but the hotels of the town were made for. Quarters were difficult to obtain, however, as a large number of contractors' men working on the new*

A photograph by W.R. Gay of South Brent of the Zulu express stranded in Brent Station, March 1891.

line of railway were residing in the place. On Monday night many passengers lay upon the floor, using their overcoats for pillows, and their rugs for coverings. A Mr Stumbles, a commercial traveller, who was one of the Brent unfortunates, gave an account of his experiences to a representative of the Western Morning News, *which has led to much subsequent controversy, and to a shower of letters, conveying many diverse opinions, being sent in to the editor of that paper. It appears that there were about forty passengers in the train, and that many of these remained at the station all night, either in the train or in the waiting-room. Next day Brent was visited, and refreshments were bought at, as Mr Stumbles says, 'famine prices'.*

The account goes on to report that:

One gentleman bought a bottle of brandy, for which he

had to pay 6s., the inns charged us double price for ordinary meals, and some establishments refused to supply us at all, probably thinking that a famine was impending. We returned to the station as best we could, through the great drifts of snow, and, with such provisions as we could buy, did the best we could, cooking such things as bloaters in the station waiting-room. Our scanty supply, I must say, was most generously supplemented from the small stores which the railway officials, such as signalmen and others, had with them. There were a number of sailors and soldiers amongst the passengers, and most of them were without means. One gentleman gave them a sovereign, and ladies from Brent also brought them money, tobacco, and provisions during our stay. On the following monotonous days we spent our time in smoking and in conversation, and also in 'chaffing' the station-master, whom we christened 'Dr Parr'. On Wednesday an enterprising amateur

Although something of a rarity, when it snows in South Brent it really snows! These two photographs were taken during the heavy snowfall of 1963. (AYRES COLLECTION)

Paul Wonnacott with his stock of secondhand cycles outside his workshop in Station Road after a particularly heavy snowfall in 1991. (WONNACOTT COLLECTION)

St Petroc's in the snow, 1984.

photographer from Brent took several views of our snowed up train, with the eighteen or twenty passengers who stuck by it perched in various prominent positions upon it. We all united in praising the minor officials, and the men in charge of the train, for remaining faithful to us, and excused the want of sympathy of 'Dr Parr' on account of his age. The driver kept the fires of his engine going all the time, but his boilers had to be filled with water by hand and in this valuable work the soldiers and marines in the train readily gave assistance. Just before we were enabled to leave Brent, we were visited for the first time by the clergyman of the parish, and our final leave-taking was celebrated by three sarcastic cheers for 'Dr Parr' and for 'Brent'. The passengers in this train included Lieutenant Rice, of the Essex Regiment, Mr R. Bayly, JP, of Plymouth (who succeeded in getting through to his home on Wednesday), Miss Sykes, and a nurse who was travelling from Scarborough to the South Devon and East Cornwall Hospital, Plymouth.

It is only fair to the station-master at Brent and to the residents of the town generally, to repeat that this description has been extensively contradicted, and among others, by Mr Robert Bayly, of Plymouth, who was another of the detained passengers. Mr Stumbles, however, has adhered to his description, and in more than one instance his version has been supported. Among other interesting details of the week in Brent, is the account of the arrival of the first newspaper, a copy

of the Western Morning News, which was brought over from Totnes on the Thursday morning by an adventurous policeman, who successfully undertook the dangerous walk. This paper was eagerly sought after, it having been the first account of the doings in the outer

William Rosamunde Gay, the photographer responsible for many of the views of Brent taken around 1900.

(CRANCH COLLECTION)

world seen since Monday, and one of the enforced sojourners in Brent is said to have paid five shillings for the use of the paper for one hour. The fortunate possessor of the journal declared that he had been offered two pounds for it, and had declined to trade.

The famous picture of the Zulu express taken by Brent photographer Mr W.R Gay is one of the last to show the old 7ft 0in. broad-gauge station.

The Coming of the Branch, 1893

We do not know how the station was laid out before 1887, although with Brent having goods facilities as well as being a passing-place for up and down trains, some sidings or loops, in addition to the two platform roads, would have been provided. The only pure broad gauge photographed is of the stranded Zulu in the blizzard of 1891.

The only record of any sort referring to Brent under South Devon Railway ownership is of an engine boiler exploding whilst a train was standing in the station. The engine, the 0–6–0 saddle tank 'Hebe', came to grief on 25 August 1873. Fortunately, no one was killed, although the driver, a fireman and a boy who was watching from the embankment were

scalded. The driver was held responsible.

In 1892, the opportunity was taken to double the line between Rattery and Hemerdon, the new line being built to the narrower standard gauge of 4ft 8in. It was necessary to widen or replace bridges because of this, including the bridge over the river just to the west of the station, while the Glazebrook viaduct was completely rebuilt. The pillars of the old viaduct can still be seen beside that which is still in use today.

At the same time as this widening and rebuilding was taking place, the construction of the branch line from Brent to Kingsbridge was finally completed. To accommodate the new junction, an entirely new station and track layout was constructed at Brent by contractors H. Lovatt. The new station cost £4,950, with other work costing an additional £3,094, and was 'fitted' between the two road bridges, 760ft apart. Although thus very compact, Brent Station had all that was needed to serve both its own area and the much larger district of Kingsbridge and the three intermediate stations at Avonwick, Gara Bridge and Loddiswell.

Completed in 1893, the new station changed little over the years. The main station building was brick-built in standard Great Western style, although the original 1891 plans provided no direct access from

Brent Station between 1893 and 1910. The station is fully operational with the branch line and goods shed in place. The sign announces that the station is the terminus for the Kingsbridge branch. On the right of the photograph is the area where the cemetery and Church Hall would be built after 1910.

Saluted by one of the railway staff, the royal train passes through Brent Station. It is possible that it was carrying King George and Queen Mary to visit Greenbank Hospital in 1915, on which occasion the Queen was presented with a posy by Brent's Mrs Amos Catt.

the main road, and passengers entered by a side gate on to the up platform and thence to the ticket office in the front. Access was from a ramp leading down from Station Road to platform level near the building, with the embankment behind coming right up to the rear of the booking-office. On a later plan, from 1894, only the roadway from Station Road appears. The road going past the station and joining up with the lower station would have been in place by 1910, when first the Village Hall, then the

Coronation Church Hall and the cemetery, were opened.

A pair of small corrugated huts were the only other buildings on the up platform. Immediately next to the entrance gate stood the stairway to the footbridge, which led across to the island platform. This, too, was a standard GW design, built of steel and corrugated iron with a roof, and was unusual in that whilst the east-facing side was open, the west-facing side was covered – Brent is famous for its rain!

The two bridges which carry the railway over the Avon, west of Brent Station. The second bridge, to the right of the photograph, was built when the second track was laid at the end of the broad-gauge era.

The building of Higher Station Bridge in 1948. Mrs Renee Cranch remembers cycling across it at the time.

(CRANCH COLLECTION)

The main supports underneath the steps were enclosed to make a coal store on the up platform and a general store on the down side. On the 550ft-long island platform, which served both the main and branch lines, opposite the main building on the up side, stood a wooden building with waiting-rooms and the usual offices. The platform was covered with a huge canopy. At the upper station bridge end was the signal-box, opened in October 1893. This was also a wooden construction, of a design known as a 'type 25'. Originally it had 61 levers, of which 10 were spares, and was supported on a raft of redun-

dant Barlow rail. As time went on the wood panelling on both the signal-box and the island platform buildings was replaced with brickwork. With the increase in passenger traffic in the early 1930s, the down platform was extended by some 60ft eastwards, whilst the up platform remained unaltered.

In 1893 a plan was mooted to make Brent into an even larger junction by running a direct line, avoiding the long inclines between Newton Abbot, Totnes and Brent, through Buckfastleigh and Ashburton to Heathfield to link up with the main line at Newton Abbot. One can only imagine just how

Brent was one of the key places for the sale of Dartmoor ponies. This picture shows ponies at Brent Station about to be sent off by rail, probably to the mines of South Wales in the early-twentieth century. (CRANCH COLLECTION)

Brent Station in the snow, 1921.

busy Brent Station would have been had this plan come to fruition.

The branch line formed a loop around the down platform, giving traffic direct access onto the main line at both ends through a system of crossovers and loops. There were sidings at both ends, enabling shunting duties on both the branch line and in the goods yard and cattle pens to be carried out efficiently, as well as allowing slower trains to be held while faster ones went through the station. At the far end of the station by Lower Station Bridge was a small loading bay where the water tower also stood.

The brick-built goods shed and the signal-box are the only two features to have survived into the twenty-first century. The goods shed had an access door for traders on its southern side, and a crane of 16-ton capacity for lifting goods. Operations were controlled from a little office on the side. The cattle pens, from which animals could be driven directly into cattle trucks at platform level, stood below the upper station bridge. This proved a popular source of entertainment for Brent children, who would sit on the wall on Brent Fair days to see the animals being loaded onto wagons to be sent to the far corners of the country.

Overlooking the station are a pair of semi-detached houses known as Balmoral Villas, reputedly built by the South Devon Railway, one of them for the station master. The 1893 trade directory for

Brent has a Dr Conran living in one of the houses, which is still known as Balmoral, while the other is called Balmoral House. The stationmaster at that time is listed as John Wilcocks, but the same directory lists 'Frederick Parr, lodging house, a stationmaster, Balmoral villa'. This was, of course, the infamous 'Dr Parr' of the 1891 stranding of the Zulu. It is not possible to say who was actually the station-master as no other records exist – the directory may have been published as a change was being made.

The Village Song-men

The Revd Sabine Baring-Gould recalls in his book *Further Reminiscences 1864–1894* visits he made to South Brent to record some folk songs as part of his collection.

A Plymouth dentist, Mr Spence Bate, who had retired from business, had a house at South Brent. He wrote to me to inform me that there were living in the place a miller, John Helmore, ruined by the setting up of a steam-mill, and a crippled stonebreaker, named Robert Hard; both notable song-men. He invited Mr Sheppard and me to pay him a visit and gather up the fragments of folk music that remained to be discovered at South Brent. Accordingly we went. It was the depth of winter, and the weather was bitter. Mr Bate's house was built over a stream from the moor, a so-called 'leet',

A steam train in the mid-twentieth century travelling around Great Aish bend towards Wrangaton, having left Brent. Brent Hill is in the background. (CRANCH COLLECTION)

and it was like an ice-house.

After dinner we adjourned to the kitchen, where was a roaring fire, and the old men were set up with jugs and tankards of ale. But some neighbouring gentlemen and ladies, notably the latter, had been invited to be present at the performance. This I saw at once would never do. Tunes have to be repeated several times to be noted with accuracy, as peasant singers are disposed to embroider them with twirls and flourishes of their own device; and further, I was not at all sure that the words of the ballads would in all cases be fit for ladies' ears. And so it proved. For after the singing of 'The Mole-Catcher' by John Helmore, the aged miller, there ensued a rapid dissolution of the company. I inserted the song in the last edition of 'Songs of the West', but to very much chastened words.

On the following day Mr Sheppard and I had the two old men to ourselves, and between us we recovered the words and airs of some very interesting pieces. In the summer I went to Mr Bate's house along with Mr Bussell, and gleaned more songs. Finally I went alone in the winter of 1890, and the Vicar of South Brent very kindly surrendered to me his drawing-room and piano, and gave me a good fire. I had in old Hard. Then and there I obtained from him a further crop of ballads. That was the last reaping, for in the ensuing bitter frost the aged man was found dead, frozen on a heap of stones by the roadside.

John Helmore, the miller, after his wife's death, ended his days in the Workhouse. I asked him one day when he began courting his 'Missus'. 'I reckon,' said he, 'when I was a baby. Us growed up together, and us

Robert Hard, one of Brent's village song-men, c.1885.

67

did ever love one another; and now her's took, please God I be took soon too, for I want to be wi' her. Us till now have niver been apart, and I du feel queer and lone at present.'

One of the songs that Robert Hard sung was 'Twas on a Sunday morning'. It was copied down in September 1889.

'Twas on a Sunday morning, before the bells did peel
A note came through my window, with Cupid for its seal
And soon I heard a whisper, as soft as breath of spring
'Twas on a Sunday morning, before the bells did ring.

The morning had been cloudy, my heart had felt the gloom
And now a sudden sunlight filled all my little room
I kissed the letter guarded with ribbons, flower and string
'Twas on a Sunday morning, before the bells did ring.

My foot the field had tarried, and on his path did rest
When in his home he caught me, and pressed me to his breast
A smile was on his fond lips, as sweet as love could bring.
'Twas on a Sunday morning, before the bells did ring.

In all, Robert Hard sang 45 songs to Revd Baring-Gould. In 1979 he was commemorated in an imaginative play written for BBC Radio Three by Sam Richards, a professional folk-singer living in Totnes. The play drew on the songs that Revd Baring-Gould copied down and on the comments of Brentonians, some of whom were descendants of Robert Hard himself and who, including the author, still live in South Brent in 2005.

Matters Medical

There has always been a medical presence in South Brent. In the 1850 directory, John Mowatt is described as the surgeon. In 1893 Richard Gillard is described as 'surgeon and medical officer and public vaccinator' for the Ugborough district of the Totnes Union. In 1902 the South Brent Nursing Association came into being and the community had its own district nurse. Its 20th Annual Report, made by Mrs Anne Collier, the secretary, on 2 June 1922 said:

The committee has much pleasure in submitting the 20th Annual report of the Association.
A total of 1,151 visits have been made and 37 maternity cases attended. The committee is pleased to be able to shew a balance of £33, due to the proceeds of two whist drives organized by a committee of which Mr H. Langler and Mr C. Goodmen were Secretaries. Had it not been for such timely help the Association must have shewn a deficit. Expenses will be heavier this year. Hitherto the S. Brent Nursing Association has paid Nurse Finnimore £80 a year, and the Devon Nursing Association has made her salary up to £120 (the

The Brent rugby team of 1901.

Brent rugby club in the early-twentieth century.

(ANDERSON COLLECTION)

minimum allowed.) In view of the fact that the Ministry of Health has reduced the yearly grant to the D.N.A. by £1200, the D.N.A. finds itself obliged to appeal to all Nursing Associations to undertake to pay their nurses an additional £10 a year as the only way to continue to help the poorer Associations. The committee has discussed the request and decided to accede to it. Therefore while heartily thanking all subscribers for their kind and continued support, an appeal is made to all residents in the district to subscribe or send a donation, however small.

The committee continued with its programme of jumble sales and concerts and was also given grants from the guardians and the Feoffees. The people of Brent paid 2d. a week to belong to the society, which remained in existence until the advent of the National Health Service in 1948.

An early Brent cricket team, pictured in the field below the railway bridge at Somerswood.

(CRANCH COLLECTION)

At the turn of the century the Devon and Cornwall authorities decided, because of the special quality and purity of the air at Didworthy, that it should become the location of a sanatorium for chest illnesses, and in 1902 the house was purchased that was to become the administrative centre for the hospital created in the vicinity.

Didworthy House was built early in the nineteenth century and Didworthy Voluntary Assisted Sanatorium opened in 1903 for the treatment of consumptives from Devon and Cornwall. A contemporary report notes:

The formal opening of the Devon and Cornwall Sanatorium for Consumptives at Didworthy, South Brent takes place today. A meeting will be held at 1.30 and two hours later the opening ceremony will be performed. An exhaustive report of the seventeen months work of the committee will be submitted, in which reference is made to the energetic efforts of Dr Clay, which were in large measure responsible for securing promises of £3,600 which enabled the committee to negotiate for the site. The Didworthy house and estate were purchased for £4,000. Mr J. Penn Milton, M.R.C.S., L.R.C.P (London) has been appointed medical officer. Six beds have been filled by poor consumptive patients, who have been sent by certain philanthropic ladies and gentlemen. Only one bed remains vacant, and it is anticipated that this bed will shortly be filled. Originally provision was only made for the reception of 14 patients; but the committee, by making certain alterations in connection with the arrangement of the staff, have been enabled to provide for two more patients. The deeds of Didworthy have been lodged with the bankers to secure the necessary overdraft. The committee trust that further donations will be forthcoming to enable the overdraft to be wiped out. Annual subscribers will also be required.

The work is now fairly started. It remains (the committee state) for the public, and in particular for those interested in the health and well-being of the poor, to provide the further funds necessary to enable the addition of 60 beds, which should be provided shortly.

For today's proceedings at Didworthy suitable trains will leave as follows: Exeter (St David's) 10.50a.m.; Plymouth (north-road) 11.45a.m.; Millbay 12.10 p.m.; and Truro, 9.20a.m.

The sanatorium comprised several blocks divided into male and female wards. In December 1909, Mr Kingwell, a former chairman of the Parish Council, attended a council meeting to express his concern that patients were frequently being seen in Brent, which he thought detrimental to the welfare of the place. This again caused concern in October of the following year, when the Parish Council sent a letter to the medical superintendent concerning the fact that patients were not being confined to the grounds of the hospital but were being allowed to visit Lutton,

Aish and Brent. The problem arose again in 1917. A new wing was opened in 1913 to accommodate ten men and the hospital was eventually transferred to local health authority control.

'Much Pleased with this Fine Church'

In 1905 Revd Howard Speare Cole became vicar of South Brent in succession to his father, William. Throughout the incumbency of both of these gentlemen the comments of successive rural deans reflect those of the Archdeacon of Totnes, who commented in 1902, 'Much pleased with this fine church which is most excellent order.' Much work was done to enhance the church at the end of the nineteenth century. Concerns were being raised in 1891 about the safety of the bells, as a result of which they were rehung by Mr Stokes of Woodbury in 1894. The same period saw several gifts to the church. The large brass eagle lectern arrived in 1894, and in 1896 Miss Ward of Lutton gave a large jewelled brass cross and Mr Stringer of Noland House donated a brass alms dish. In 1898 the organ was enlarged and restored by Hele & Co. and a service to mark its 'opening' was held by the Archdeacon of Totnes on Friday 15 April 1898. Work to improve the heating was undertaken in 1902 and, while there were

The eagle lectern in St Petroc's. The eagle was considered to be the highest flying bird and so the Bible rested on its wings. (ADDY COLLECTION)

Arthur Hard, William Knapman, Phil Luscombe, Harry Cole, Richard Veale, Bert Luscombe and Lily and Charles Goodman outside the Anchor Hotel on 22 June 1911, the day of the coronation of King George V and Queen Mary. (ANDERSON COLLECTION)

suggestions of placing a screen across the tower arch as early as 1903, it was not until 1906 that a curtain was put there instead. Gas lighting arrived in 1908 and was very favourably received.

The Revd William Rankin Dunlop Elwell was instituted to the benefice of South Brent on 26 April 1920. His wife, Emilie Elwell, was the patron of the parish and it was during his incumbency that the Ecclesiastical Commissioners for England consented to the sale of part of the South Brent glebe lands – lands traditionally part of the benefice of the parish and for the benefit of the vicar. The house at the bottom of Church Street now known as Marlborough House, along with its outbuildings and land (with the exception of the vicar's hall and the field below Splatton known as Hazeland) were sold to Mr Francis Weymouth. Another area of glebe land was sold to the Parochial Church Council for the provision of additional burial-grounds, which were brought into use in 2001.

Elwell's son, Clarence Elwell, became vicar of the parish in 1923. This meant that from 1845 the incumbency of South Brent had been held by only two families. It was in 1925 that parts of the old rood-screen that had been removed in 1870 were restored to the church in the form of altar rails at the high altar and an altar table for the war memorial. It was Revd Clarence Elwell who was to preside over an interesting occurrence, of which more later.

The Coronation of King George V, 1911

The coronation of King George V on 22 June 1911 was a day of celebration in South Brent. A committee was set up to oversee the arrangements, with Mr

The opening of the Coronation Church Hall in 1911.

The Village Hall.

Wyndham Hull as secretary and treasurer.

At 8a.m. there was a peal of church bells prompting the population to hoist flags as early as possible. At 11.30a.m. there was a service at St Petroc's and a United Nonconformist service in the Wesleyan Chapel in Church Street. At a general gathering around the jubilee lamp at 1.30p.m. the assembled company sang the National Anthem, and there followed a procession to the sports and tea field (the vicarage lawn) for the sports to commence. The inevitable public tea for the under 13s began at 4p.m., with high tea for those over 13 years at 5p.m. For both events participants had to bring their own crockery and cutlery. An alfresco dance was held at 6p.m. with further celebrations in the evening. The day's celebrations culminated in a grand bonfire on Brent Hill.

The First World War

One of the most significant international events to affect Brent in the turbulent twentieth century was the First World War.

After the end of the war it was proposed that a

memorial be erected in memory of the fallen. A meeting was held in September 1919 to decide how best this should be achieved, with a committee formed, 'those elected being men who have "done their bit" and worn the King's uniform during the war', and 31 other worthies. The chairman of the Parish Council, Mr E.W. Mead, suggested a children's playing-field. Mr R.H. Gill, whilst agreeing with Mr Mead, proposed that a public park would be preferable as it could be self-sustaining in financial terms and be a good asset for the 'health and amusement' of the people of Brent. Mr Hosking of Brent Mill proposed the construction of a 50ft tower on the top of Brent Hill with 'the names of all the boys engraven in the side thereof'. He also suggested that those who had 'escaped the Army could well be expected to pay £25 towards it in gratitude to those who had been taken never to return.' This idea did not find a seconder, and it was suggested that the names could as easily be engraved on a stone in the cemetery or in the proposed public park.

At the Vestry meeting in 1920 the vicar was able to announce that 'the war memorial committee had collected about £100 and it was intended to erect a marble war shrine in the church.'

Thus a war memorial was placed inside St Petroc's across the north door. Part of the former rood-screen was used as the base for an altar table and the names of the fallen were inscribed on the marble plaque placed above it.

Some interesting facts have been discovered about some of those fought in the war. The author's cousin, Mark Simmons, has researched the record of their grandfather, Alfred Scott Hard. He writes:

Members of my family used to say my maternal Grandfather had 'gone missing in the Dardanelles during the Great War'. Grandfather joined the Royal Marines on June 18, 1897. It may have been the

John Piper during the First World War.

Ernest Salter, who was killed in action during the First World War.

Alfred Scott Hard in the uniform of the Marines. He went missing in the Dardanelles during the First World War.

celebrations for Queen Victoria's Diamond Jubilee that year that galvanised him into joining up.

His first service was with the Plymouth Division. Later he served on the China Station aboard the first-class battleship HMS Victorious. In 1910 grandfather returned to the colours after being invalided out in 1907 and on 3 April was enrolled in the Royal Fleet Reserve. His last training stint with the Fleet Reserve was 15–25 July 1914. On 3 August 1914, with war looming, he joined HMS Ocean, the fifth of six Canopus battleships. On 11 September 1914, the Ocean left Plymouth for the Mediterranean and Persian Gulf. She arrived off the Dardanelles in February 1915. The ship was then involved in the first all-out attack on the narrows to allow the fleet to pass through. Although the area had been regularly swept of mines, the Turks had laid a small minefield which caused many ships, including the Ocean to come to grief. Our grandfather was transferred to Ark Royal, eventually serving in HMS

James 'Jim' White of the Devonshire Regiment, who died on 23 June 1918, aged 27. (SANDRY COLLECTION)

Top and above: *Prisoners of war at Brentmoor House in 1917.* (CRANCH COLLECTION)

Edgar *until 1917. He returned to Brent, where he died in 1935. Royal Marines carried his coffin at the funeral.*

Similarly, Mrs Renee Cranch's father, John Piper, went missing during the war. More recollections of similar adventures, now lost to posterity, were no doubt recounted by those men and women who returned.

During the First World War the bell-ringers recorded in their Ringers' Book:

In view of the Great War and taking into consideration the seriousness of the situation, the Ringers thought that it would not be in unison with our forces at the front to hold the annual supper. Therefore it was unanimously decided to abandon the idea until another year or such other time when the country shall be at peace.

Even so, the ringers met throughout the war to elect their lord chief and crier. In 1914 the posts fell to G. Turpin and J. Cole.

The Formation of the WI

In November 1920 the first meeting took place of one of the village's oldest societies, the Women's Institute. In 1980 the WI produced a booklet, *Sixty Years within South Brent.*

There were 66 ladies present at the public meeting on 27 October 1920 at which it was decided that a Women's Institute should be formed. At the first meeting, in November 1920, those attending heard about the work of the WI from a member of the newly formed Ivybridge WI, and the South Brent branch has since grown and flourished, even through the difficult war years.

The early meetings of South Brent WI were held in the Church Hall and the annual membership fee was 2s., which members could choose to pay in two equal instalments. In January 1921 Mrs C. Arnold, the second president, donated a hut for meetings, for which a suitable site on the left-hand side of Springfield Road, at a ground rent of £2.2s., was eventually found in a field owned by Mrs H. Mahon. The hut was officially opened on 12 October 1921, a year after the formation of the Institute, and was shared with the Girl Guides, who had a separate room for their meetings.

At the first meetings in the hut, members had to provide their own chair and, as there was no piano,

The interior of the WI hut.   (INEZ JORDAN COLLECTION)

one was borrowed for social events until it was decided that the WI should have its own. With no money to spare, a piano fund was set up and a concert raised enough for a piano to be bought in 1923 for £31.10s, the payment being made in several instalments. WI members were charged 6d. to practise on the piano, while other organisations using the hut were charged 15s. with use of the piano and 7s.6d. without.

General meetings were held on the last Wednesday of every month, with the committee also meeting monthly. It was quite common for a committee meeting to be called to discuss a special subject, and only one or two meetings were abandoned for lack of a quorum. From August 1921 until the present time, meetings have been held on the first Wednesday in the month.

Most early WI meetings seem to have had the same format as those of today – a speaker would talk on a topic of interest, then there were popular short courses which included basket making, canework, rug making, cookery, easy pottery, lampshade making, slipper and wedge-heel making and even thatching. Indeed, according to records, members could at one time take part in basket making on Wednesdays, acting on Thursdays and needlework and stitchery on Fridays. Of course, there were also the competitions, a notable one being to cook a dinner for four at a cost of no more than 2s. All this, plus a mountain of other interesting things to do, at a time when women had fewer opportunities to escape their environment.

Another feature of the yearly programmes was a garden party in June or July, at which members enjoyed their afternoon meeting as guests at one of the larger houses in Brent. Over a cup of tea served in the garden, members could sit and talk or wander and admire the shrubs and flower-beds. After tea, business would be discussed and then a competition or treasure hunt for hidden parcels would round off the afternoon's enjoyment. No woman was excluded from any meeting and members could bring a guest. In the early years a by-law was passed in Brent WI 'that each member may bring one friend to one meeting a year for free, subsequent guests to be charged sixpence.'

The first WI flower and produce show took place in 1921 and members have continued to support numerous such exhibitions over the years. To enter produce into these early shows – and there was always a formidable number of entries – cost 6d. Shows were kept open until late evening to allow 'cottagers' to view after a day's work. Whist drives proved a very popular way of raising funds, in fact it was quite common when funds were low for a whist drive to be organised quickly, charging 2s.6d. per head including refreshments. Back in the 1920s sports were held that included events for all ages, with prizes ranging from 3d. to 1s.6d. Children of members paid a penny to enter an event, while the children of non-members paid 3d. The popular summer picnics usually enjoyed fine weather.

The annual harvest supper started in 1927 with cold beef and ham on the menu and, with the exception of one year during the war, has been held every year since, the members organising the whole event.

One of the aims of the WI is to help and encourage a better, healthier life for everyone. In April 1921 it was proposed to set up an infant welfare centre and a baby show was arranged with entrants charged 4d.

(non-members 6d.) for every baby entered. There were 31 entries. The clinic was started in the early 1930s, with tea provided by the WI. During the war years the food executive office gave a permit to obtain one pint of milk and one quarter of tea for use at the clinic twice a month.

Disaster at Manor Mills

In November 1923 there was a disastrous fire at Manor Mills. A contemporary account describes the events:

When the foreman of Messrs Clatworthy & Co.'s manor Flock Mills went on duty at 6a.m. yesterday he was attracted by the smell of burning rags and discovered the higher part of the drying shed to be ablaze. He took prompt effort to extinguish the fire but without success and before the Brent fire engine arrived the whole roof fell in. The brigade directed their attention to the southern end of the building where nearly £2,000 was recently spent in a new and powerful engine for working the tearing machines. This was fortunately saved from much damage but all the remaining part of the building was totally destroyed.

The disinfecting and drying machines at the mills are worked day and night except on Sunday nights and it is believed the fire was caused by combustion when the plant was not working.

The manager of the mills at the time was Mr Goss, while Captain Parnell was in command of the fire-engine. This, at the time being in poor condition, Mr Goss saved the day by cutting the end of a water launder and turning the full force of the mill leat on the fire, preventing it from spreading to the main building, where there was flock awaiting dispatch. Mr Clatworthy visited the scene the following day and arranged for the reconstruction of the damaged buildings.

Two further mills are mentioned in some sources, one of them at Horsebrook. In 1688 Richard Prowse, a yeoman, is said to have taken over a dwelling-house and mills. He still, however, had to bring his corn to be processed at Brent Mill.

A Plan to Revive China Clay Workings

In 1923 there were high hopes that the old workings of the Dartmoor China Clay Works at Shipley would be successful. In June it was reported that:

During the past five weeks a considerable amount of pioneering work has been accomplished and already the output has reached about 40 tons per week while a dozen workers are employed.

After over 40 years idleness these old works have been restarted along with new pits on the eastern side of the old pits at Yellowbrook, while the 'prospectors' have

met with a promising yield in the vicinity of Whitebarrow.

The manager of the undertaking, a St Austell man, who has been brought up in the midst of the china clay industry, is doing his utmost to make the scheme a success. He has secured an area of about 15 square miles on lease for 40 years and when the work is further advanced it is expected that over 1000 tons of clay per week will be processed.

Engineers who have visited the scene of the operations have expressed surprise at the manner in which the work has been advanced within the short period of five weeks. Already the 'milky way' has appeared on the moorside, where the channels with the clay in liquid provide miniature cascades until the liquid reaches the series of pits or filter beds. Everything is being done to minimize pollution of adjacent waterways but it is contended that the filtered solution is harmful to fish

The promoters of the scheme have been fortunate in finding the old lines of pipes which led the liquid from the pits to Shipley drying sheds. Except in places where rabbits have played havoc with the aqueduct, the pipe line is in a state of good repair. Workmen are being kept busy repairing the pipe track which extends over four miles over the moorland and also the various pits at Shipley.

About 300 tons of clay are under cover and as the work advances the tall square granite chimney stack, which has been a familiar landmark in the vicinity of Shipley for several decades will be brought into use, while the adjacent drying sheds, drying apparatus and the old stores will be reconstructed.

The contractor has been fixed for the introduction of motor transport to handle the clay from Shipley to Brent (Station). According to the promoters, the quality of the clay is equal to the best placed on the market and they are hopeful that a large number of extra men will be required in connection with this devilment of the industry in Devonshire.

Brentmoor House and 'The Children of Men'

In 1923 Brent featured in the works of another famous author. Eden Phillpotts chose to set the last of his Dartmoor cycle of novels in the Avon valley and particularly at Brentmoor House, which for the purposes of the story was renamed The Red House. The story revolves around the Bullstone family. Kate van der Kiste writes of the house, which she knew well:

Built in the early part of the 19th century for wealthy land owner Mr Meynell, it was a beautiful granite house, large and solid, with slate roof, part slate-hung walls, mullioned windows, and a sprawling collection of outbuildings including cow sheds, dairy, stables, servants' quarters, a small cottage, and dog kennels. Mr Meynell tried to enclose the greater part of Brent

Brentmoor House in the early-twentieth century. The turret housed the bathroom. (CRANCH COLLECTION)

Brentmoor House in the winter of 1934.
(VAN DER KISTE COLLECTION)

Moor, but opposition from the Commoners caused him to abandon the project: the remains of a reave, known as Meynell's Bank, can still be traced in the area of Whitebarrow and Knattabarrow.

On a rocky outcrop just inside and to the left of the main gate, stands a small memorial to 'M.M.', complete with a typically sentimental Victorian verse:

My lovely little lily
Thou wert gathered very soon,
In the fresh and dewy morning
Not in the glare of noon.
The Saviour sent his angels
To bear thee hence, my own.
And they'll plant thee in that garden
Where decay is never known.

This was erected in memory of Margaret, the Meynell's small daughter who died of a childhood complaint on March 27th 1865. Rumour has it that the snow was so thick on the roads at the time, that they were unable to get the body to Brent for burial, and that she is actually buried at that spot, though this seems unlikely. At one time the stone was set in a pretty little bower, with a garden and lily-pond, but now the rhododendrons have taken over and one has to bend almost double to read the inscription.

Prior to the Great War the house was leased to Rear Admiral John Tuke, and in those days was fully staffed inside and out. The gardens were beautifully kept, the stables full of horses, and each day the postman would ride out early from Brent with the mail, to be rewarded with breakfast in the big back kitchen. The entrance porch, which was a room in itself, was used for household prayers and even Sunday services on occasions, a footman providing music for the hymns on a tissue-paper covered comb! Since there was no bathroom, and water had to be pumped by hand, hip-baths were the order of the day or week. Later a bathroom was added, but as the room had no outside walls a little turret with

windows was built up to let in the light, and this was a most attractive feature of the place. The plumbing was erratic to say the least of it, and the outside thunder-box was far more convenient than the inside mod. con.

The next tenant was William Ambrose Pritchard, a rich eccentric, who had travelled widely, and claimed never to have done a stroke of work in his life. His idea was to settle down and indulge his fancy for breeding Irish terriers. Anyone who has read Eden Philpotts's Children of Men will recognise him as Jacob Bullstone, and Brentmoor as The Red House.

It was in 1929 that we made the acquaintance of the family, as the Pritchard children, John and Barbara, were the same age as my brother and I, and during the next ten years we grew to love the house and its surroundings. I can sit now on a stone which was once on the front-door step and see it just as it was in those days of childhood before the Second World War. I must have sat in just that spot many times, shelling peas, or beans, with Pam, the sole remaining Irish terrier stretched out on the warm stone in the sunshine. Did the sun always shine when we were young?

At the front Mr Pritchard had made a lovely garden of sunken paths and flower-beds raised almost to chest height. He was enormously fat and could not bend, so this was the answer to his horticultural problems. At the back was a large vegetable garden, enclosed by iron railings to keep out marauding sheep and cattle, and on the opposite side of the river another kitchen garden was reached by a footbridge made from seven pine trees. Though he could keep out the cattle, he could not do the same to the cabbage white butterflies, and would pay us 6d. a hundred for their caterpillars in a jam jar. Adults often found him anti-social and cantankerous, but to us he was 'Uncle Billy' who always had a tin of Old English Humbugs in his study, lent us books and ponies, and let us listen to his wireless.

As well as Irish terriers, he had a herd of Dartmoor ponies; one lovely dark brown foal called Dusky he gave to my younger sister. He also bred tiny Dexter cattle

A derelict Brentmoor House before it was destroyed by the Royal Marines in the 1960s.

which we were allowed, nay encouraged, to milk; the little black bull was called Johnny Boulder, and our favourite cow was Granny. In addition to a motley assortment of dogs, cats and chickens, there was an African grey parrot who lived in the kitchen and spent her days mimicking members of the family.

On fine days there were enormous picnics on the flat rocks beside the bathing pool, friends walking or riding up from miles around. Sometimes there would be 20 or 30 people, plus dogs and ponies, and in the evening we would gather round the piano in the drawing-room, singing or listening to the playing of Mrs Pritchard, who was an accomplished musician.

The house had to have a ghost, and Brentmoor's was that of a nurse-maid who had smothered her charge, and in a fit of remorse threw herself in the river. People who slept in the room where the deed was committed were said to wake up with a feeling of imminent suffocation.

The house, once so full of life, had a melancholy end. Driven from home by their father's domineering personality, John joined the RAF in 1939 – it was he who introduced me to my future husband – and Barbara went into the WAAF. Mrs Pritchard left to live with her sister. Eden Philpotts's book, though written some 20 years earlier, was strangely prophetic. Alone, unloved, and a very sick man, 'Uncle Billy' soon died in the great empty house, and one wet miserable day, his possessions, trophies from all over the world, beautiful antiques and pictures, were sold by auction.

The Youth Hostel Association then took over, and later, with the Avon Dam under construction, it was used by the SWWB as offices and accommodation, becoming more and more dilapidated and vandalised, until finally the Royal Marines blew up what was left as a field exercise.

This article previously appeared in
Devon Life, *February 1980.*

At School in the 1920s and '30s

Mr A. Baker became head teacher of Brent School in October 1923 and remained in charge until September 1930, at which time various county staff took over until the arrival of 'Boss' Symons in June of 1931.

Some of those who received their early education at the school rose to hold such posts as chairman of BOAC (British Overseas Airways Corporation), as well as high positions in the police, in the teaching and nursing professions and in the services. Here are some reminiscences of a pupil at South Brent Council School, as it was known in its early days, in the late 1920s and early 1930s:

The school was a happy place and the managers would walk around to see that everything was as it should be. In the 1920s children stayed at Brent School from the age of five right up until 14. Often they were taken at the age of three if they would settle down. There were six classes and a family atmosphere where the older members looked after the younger. The three Rs were the chief subjects and the day always started with Scripture lessons when each class sang a hymn. Then certain classes went into the playground for keep fit, the boys in one playground and the girls in the other. Arithmetic came next, starting with tables or mental arithmetic and then the break. In cold weather or wet weather people would try to congregate around one of the big black combustion stoves. It was very cold at the other end of the room. Children would wait until the teacher had disappeared and then trip back into class early to warm up. After a break would come reading, writing and composition. Then nearly all the children that lived in the town would go home to dinner when the bell rang. Pupils who came in from Avonwick, Rattery, (where the school had been closed in 1923 because of its poor condition), and the outlying hamlets and farms, would have their packed lunches. The monitors would be sent to make cocoa. These children either walked to school or rode ponies which were stabled at the Pack Horse or in a friendly farmer's field during school hours. In later years taxis brought children to and from school as they do now.

After lunch for the first part of the afternoon it was history or geography and then the boys and girls in the class would break up. The boys would go with the male teachers and the girls with the female ones. This meant cookery or needlework for the girls and many tears were shed over sewing the sides of pillowslips. The stitches had to be the same length. In the end it was rewarding to take a rather grey pillowslip home for mother to buy. The boys worked in the woodwork room with their tools. There must have been many stools, coat-hangers, racks and pipe-hangers around that were made at that time. Sometimes they went gardening in the school gardens opposite the station.

In July 1920 it was reported to the Brent Feoffees that the boys' garden of instruction was to be sold. In October of the same year it was decided to transfer such funds from the educational portion of the charity as were necessary to meet the increase in rent brought about by allowing gardening instruction for the boys to continue.

Games were played in the afternoons and in 1924 the Brent Feoffees granted £3 for the rental of a field for the purpose, provided that the children were supervised and that permission was granted by the newly formed cricket club for the use of the field. In 1928 the grant was increased to £8. Also in 1924, the trustees provided 10 capes for the use of the boys in wet weather, whilst in 1925 they gave a gift of £3.9s.8d. so that the children could journey by railway to Exeter to take part in a class singing competition.

One school record concerns an occasion when there was a Scripture exam in progress. All was quiet. The children were busily writing. Suddenly there was a commotion outside the school and the caretaker burst into the room crying, 'Quick, quick, there is a fire up to Aish.' All the children immediately trooped out to watch it. There were not many passes that year!

There was another incident, this time in the school garden, where there happened to be some good apple trees. Two boys climbing over the cemetery wall to scrump some apples were seen by another pupil. When confronted the boys' excuse was that they had carried some suitcases from the station for a lady and she had given them some apples. When the headmaster asked who, then, had broken into the school gardens, the pair had to own up and were given six of the best on each hand.

One further recollection is of a scare in Church Street, when a three-year-old girl went missing when the time came to go back to school. Police and neighbours spent two hours searching everywhere, until

Brent School, c.1930. Left to right, back row: Fred Burrows, Bill Hannaford, ?, ?, Ken Fox, Fred Retter, Cliff Pulleyblank; second row: Joan Quirk, Maureen Hard, Beryl Harris, Brenda Coaker, Barbara Sleep, Frances Luscombe, Maisie Luscombe, Hilda Quirk, Barbara Lang, Gwen May; front row: Eddie Sowden, Edgar Male, Bernie Retter, ? Hobbs.

A trip to the seaside. (HONEYWILL COLLECTION)

the child's older sister, on returning home from school, went into the sitting-room and found two little feet sticking out from underneath the tablecloth. The little girl had not wandered far!

At the end of the school year all the children looked forward to the Sunday-school outing, which always took place on the first Wednesday of the holidays. Both Anglicans and Methodists would hire coaches on the ten o'clock train to Teignmouth. The 'church children' would line up along the cemetery side of the station entrance, and the 'chapel children' by the railway buildings. They would then troop into the reserved coaches; buckets and spades in hand. Their parents would then be allowed onto the platform to buy their tickets.

The Dramatic Tradition Begins

There has long been a tradition for amateur theatricals in Brent. It was all begun nearly 100 years ago by Arthur Manning, as Maggie Taylor records in her unpublished record of the South Brent Amateur Dramatic Society (SBADS). Many people in South

Charles Tothill's 1950 production of Aladdin, *featuring Elizabeth Knapman as Aladdin, George Salter as Widow Twankey, with Reg Edgecombe, William Windeatt, Owen Winzer, Reg Rave, Harry Westcott and Russell Chulk.*

(INEZ JORDAN COLLECTION)

The Sleeping Beauty, *1949, featuring David Grigor and June Andrews.* (PARSONS COLLECTION)

Brent remember Mr Manning as a master musician who had his own dance band and who was also involved with other musical groups. Many older Brentonians knew him as the church organist and choirmaster at St Petroc's Church. Although blind, he knew by the sounds of the voices exactly where each of his choristers was sitting. The author can well remember, that while sitting in choir practice on an evening in November, the young choirboys changed places during rehearsals of 'A Virgin Unspotted'. By the end of the carol Mr Manning knew exactly where each of them was and they never changed places again.

In 1925 he founded the drama group which was later to evolve into SBADS. The original intention was to stage a pantomime for the Sunday-school outings fund with the first production, *Beauty and the Beast*, being staged on Boxing Day 1926, with Theo Preston as the Beast. Mr Manning then went on to produce many shows, always expecting the highest standards from his cast, including the children who featured in his pantomimes and are today still prominent in Brent productions.

On stage in the Church Hall for Cinderella. *Left to right:* George Westcott, George Salter, Alma Preston, William Windeatt, Christine Preston, Pam Andrews, Margaret O'Shea *and* Mrs Deedes.

The cast of Dick Whittington, *of which the newspapers reported that, 'The show was written and produced by Edward Rowe, who liberally embellished his dialogue with delightfully topical digs at the innumerable problems of the present day. A chorus of pretty girls provided a touch of sophistication for the adult patrons, whilst the artless simplicity of the tiny fairies soon had the audience captivated.'* (INEZ JORDAN COLLECTION)

Brent Outings

Church outing in July 1972 in one of Hard's Coaches. Those pictured include Revd Malsom, Ruth Hard, Julie Towl, Olive Mortimore, Edie Davis, Les Hard, Pauline Towl, Angela Vallance, Louise Handsford, Collette Crosbie. (VALLANCE COLLECTION)

A Co-op outing to Burnham-on-Sea with, left to right, Pat Crosbie, Robin Maddock, Bing Crosbie, Margaret Newman, Margaret O'Shea, Ann Hayman, Brenda Newman and Nano O'Connell.

A Sunday-school outing to Teignmouth, 1972. Left to right, back row: Ken Fox, Andrew Fox, Emma O'Shea Collette, Violet Fox, Mrs O'Connell; front row: Collette Crosbie, Simon Fox, a visitor from London, Dennis Wood, Nano Wood (née O'Connell). (WOOD COLLECTION)

Charabanc trips early in the twentieth century. (INEZ JORDAN COLLECTION)

CHAPTER 6

The Brock Era, 1927–54

An aerial view of South Brent as it was in 1952. The railway line and station in the foreground will bring back many memories of local travel. Note the jubilee lamppost in the centre of the square. (AEROFILMS LTD)

Brent Fair between the Wars

Mrs Sheila Wall (great grand-daughter of Robert Hard, one of the village song-men) recorded her reminiscences of what it was like to live in Church Street at the time of the fair. Mrs Wall was born in one of the cottages in Church Street in 1921 and grew up with the fair from childhood.

Folks would be looking forward to the fair for weeks. When the travellers came out to Broadimoor or down to Bunny Andrews's field where Avondale is now with their horses and caravans with their dogs following, we knew that it would soon be time for the fair. The women would come around selling pegs and suchlike. They carried their babies on their backs, which must have

been uncomfortable for the child. Their other children would come with them. They would knock on the door and ask my mother if she wanted anything or to have her fortune told. Nobody would refuse.

The night before the fair proper was very busy. The lord of the manor's men brought the hurdles up from the hurdle house in Millswood Lane and they would make pens with them over in the church car park. John Maye's little box would be down in Wellington Square and John Pearce's over by the Vicar's Hall at the bottom of Church Street near to where the Police Station was. The policemen inside the Police Station used to sit in their shirt sleeves but if anything went wrong then on would go their tunics and helmets and they would be out. One fair day, a traveller who had had too many drinks and was a bit worse for it was put in the cells, the wash house in fact. When the police came to see how he was, he'd escaped and made tracks before anyone knew anything about it.

On the morning of the fair, the white glove was put out on the Toll House and any animals passing would have to pay a toll.

Us children had a day off from school and were up very early. We would have to wear Wellington boots and carry a stick. Barricades were put up to all downstairs windows and across the courts. Big boxes were put outside Charlie White, the butcher's and Bully Walke, the saddler's.

Early in the morning the sheep started coming at about 4 o'clock. They were driven. The pigs came in a horse-drawn cart that had a net thrown over the top.

By the time they started to sell the cattle the pubs were open. It was one of the days when people would see a lots of people they knew but may not have seen for some time so they would wet their whistles in the Anchor or the Royal Oak. The travellers liked the Pack Horse. Charlie Clitson was the landlord of the Pack Horse and as he'd been a boxer in his time he wouldn't have any nonsense. If things started getting out of hand he knew how to deal with them.

Gill's potato and meat pasties made a nice bite to eat at dinner time. The cattle made their way up to the station to be taken away and us children used to go up and sit on the wall to see them being loaded.

The horses were sold around two o'clock. The farmers had had plenty of time to view by then. The travellers would try out their horses along Plymouth Road. It is said that one farmer bought a horse from a traveller, put it in his field and when he came to look for him the next day he had disappeared without trace. The moor ponies were in little groups up by Higher Station Bridge. The shire horses looked lovely parading in Station Road with their brasses sparkling and shining.

After the cattle had gone from down in Church Street, out came the disinfectant to get everything clean again. I think the disinfectant was pink. The water came from the fire hydrants. The children used to go down to the fairground. There were roundabouts and swing boats and all sorts of side shows. I can remember one girl had such a good time that she lost her shoe and found it in the field next door on the following day. At the end of the day we started looking forward to the next Brent Fair.

The custom of holding the fair in the streets ceased after the Second World War and the selling of stock was moved to the Sheep Field. In 1936 the sheep sale was held on 24 August. Local reports tell us that:

Bidding was brisk and prices were generally good, but although 44 registered rams from the South Devon Flock were offered for sale only 14 were bought, the top price being 12½ guineas. Registered rams of the Dartmoor Sheepbreeders and Flockbook Association were offered to the number of 76 and of these 35 were

sold, the top price being 17½ guineas, the auctioneer was John Maye. In total 1182 breeding ewes averaged 59/5d, 91 wethers averages 42/5d and 200 lambs averaged 35/4d against 33/- the previous year. The top price for ewes was 78/- from Mr W. Cleeve of Stidston.

South Brent Primary School

Mr H.G. Symons became headmaster of South Brent Primary School in June 1931 and remained until the end of the 1938/39 academic year. He had the reputation amongst his pupils, who named him 'the Boss', of being very strict.

In 1936 he asked for a grant from the Feoffees to purchase an epidiascope, which at that time cost about £25, 'as an important and useful aid to education in the present progressive age.' Although some of the trustees were of the opinion that this should be provided by the County Education Committee, they voted that the equipment should be purchased. In June, a meeting of the trustees was held in the school to 'examine the use of the provided epidiascope'. There is no comment as to their conclusions!

In 1933 the Feoffees recommended the foundation of a special evening class to be taught by the headmaster 'with a view to extra instruction of a few boys about to leave school in the hope they may be fit to undergo examination for appointments about the end of May.' For this the trustees decided to allow payment of £4.4s.0d.

In April 1937 the money granted by the Feoffees for the use of the school was used for:

1. Cocoa and milk for hot drinks at School for children who dine at school.
2. Papers or magazines suitable for children's use same time in school.
3. Assistance to school library upkeep.
4. Assistance towards Playing Fields – County Council Field now available.
5. Gym shoes for children's drill and exercise. (Capes or mackintoshes no longer required.)
6. Garden rent (£6) and manure (£1).
7. Epidiascope maintenance and improvement.
8. Educational Music (Choir for adults at 1s.6d. per practice in the school).
9. Evening School instruction (if classes held) and assistance to keep fit endeavours.

In considering these items, it was proposed by two of the Feoffees, General Armstrong and the chairman, and subsequently agreed, to:

... invite the headmaster (Mr Symons) to come along to a future Meeting of the Trustees with view to showing the Trustees the necessity of such charitable grants in the future.

In 1938 the County Council took over the provision

South Brent handbell ringers in the 1950s. Left to right, standing: *John Piper, Eric Rush, George Wilkinson, ?, Harry Soper, Hugh Butler;* seated: *Julian Deedes, Mary Honeywell, Rose Luggar, Mrs Butler, Norman Hard.*

(Cranch Collection)

of rent for the school garden. The headmaster requested that the amount of money which had been granted annually from the Feoffees for the purpose of renting the land should be transferred to library use. The trustees agreed to his request but wished to inspect the contents of the library annually to check that the materials were appropriate.

Many schoolchildren in those days had jobs before and after school. Bert Field can remember delivering milk for Bert Foale before school. He had a milk cooler in a pram and measuring jugs were hung on the side to measure the milk straight into the customer's jug.

1927 – Ringers' Strike

Unidentified newspaper cuttings around Sunday 24 April 1927 record the events surrounding the ringers' 'strike' of 1927, describing it as a 'Real Life Comedy at South Brent'.

The root of the problem which caused all the ringers to resign can be traced back to 4 November 1926, when the annual dinner of the ringers was held in accordance with tradition, the lord chief for the year was elected and the Ringers' Book was signed. On this occasion Mr A.W. Cranch, one of the church-wardens, presented the ringers with a set of eight handbells complete with a glass-fronted wooden case and a key, all of which had been purchased by public subscription.

Mr Wilkinson, the lord chief, took charge of the key after the presentation and for a month the ringers practised on the handbells 'and attained a moderate proficiency'.

At the December meeting of the Parochial Church Committee the members decided that the right and proper place for the handbell key was on the sexton's bunch, and secretary Mr Wyndham Hull wrote to Mr Wilkinson asking him to return it. Mr Wilkinson sent the key back as requested but the ringers considered that as the handbells had been presented to them

South Brent bell-ringers first team, 1995. Left to right, back row: *Ray Mugridge, Neil Holloway, Ray Wakeley;* front row: *Charlie Hard, Linda Newman, Trevor Newman.*

(Bell-ringers Collection)

The South Brent handbells.   (ADDY COLLECTION)

they should be the ones to hold the key. Such was their dissatisfaction that they decided to ring no more. This action was considered to be a strike.

In fairness to the ringers it should be said that it was no such thing. If they wanted to strike they could have struck last Christmas when the trouble arose, but they waited quite properly and constitutionally until Easter – the end of the church year – and then handed in their resignations in a body.

The churchwardens, who had been told there would be no ringing on Sunday, were unable to placate the ringers. At a special meeting of the Church Council the ringers were asked to attend and state their grievance. Mr R.H. Gill, one of the churchwardens, said:

We are very proud of our bells and of our ringers. We have done everything to encourage the ringers and when they expressed a desire for a set of handbells we opened a subscription and found the money. I don't think they are expressing their gratitude very well in the action they have taken. If they had made their grievances known we could have rectified it.

The Vicar [Revd C. Elwell] said he knew nothing officially of the matter. All he could say was that the ringers had certainly not rung the bells on Sunday for some reason of their own. He would not call the affair a 'strike' preferring the term 'misunderstanding'. He anticipated that the matter would be settled in the course of a week or so.

And the Church Itself...

In 1931 Revd William Kilbridge Gallagher became vicar of South Brent. Throughout the 1930s the comments about St Petroc's are generally good. Some concern was raised about the yew trees in the churchyard but there were none of the criticisms of a century earlier. The Revd H.R. Evans, the rural dean of Totnes, when he visited the church in March 1932 commented, 'that there is considerable evidence of care being taken to the improvement of the churchyard and the maintenance of the church fabric.'

A new altar was installed during 1933. In 1934 a significant change took place when the old stone pulpit was converted into stairs for the vestry and a new wooden pulpit of carved oak, costing £228, was put in its place. The pulpit was given in memory of Mr Prince of Somerswood and was similar to the carved oak choir stalls and organ screen designed by Hems of Exeter and placed in the church in 1926 in memory of George Vere Hugh Cholmondeley of Glazebrook. The installation of the new pulpit gave 50 men work over a period of nine months. At the same time the Lady Chapel was restored and furnished with new silvered altar furniture. During this period various other gifts were given to the church in the form of offertory boxes and collection bags and in 1935 an icon was placed in the Lady Chapel. At this time the tradition of placing flowers in the church windows was introduced. In 2005 three of the windows had flowers placed in them by the same families as 70 years before. Electric lighting was also installed.

In 1937 concerns were raised about the state of the bells, which were described by the rural dean, Revd John Martin, as being 'dangerous' and would cost £300 to repair. The work was done and the bells were rededicated on 3 November when Mr M. Elliott was the lord chief, so that in 1938 the rural dean comments: 'This is now a magnificent church and the great effort to rehang the bells has been successful.' The rural dean suggested that the next project might be the replacement of the pitch-pine pews with oak ones 'more in keeping with the building'.

In 1945 Revd Ivor K. Jones became vicar of South Brent and it is during his incumbency that another

Revd William Kilbridge Gallagher, vicar 1931–45.

(CRANCH COLLECTION)

The church fête of Wednesday 29 June 1932. A highlight of the summer, the church fête was held on alternate Wednesdays (early-closing day) and Saturdays in the grounds of the vicarage.
(CRANCH COLLECTION)

A church fête at the vicarage, c.1959.

(WILD COLLECTION)

Messrs Bill Endacott, Jimmy Garland, Frank Rawlings and Frank Watts at a church fête in the vicarage garden in the 1950s. Mr Watts was the sexton of the churchyard for many years, and his wife was the caretaker of the church hall.

St Petroc's Church fête, 2003. The picture includes Eileen Grills, Moray Vorster, Lindy Brierly, Judith Morris (seated) and Stephen Morris.

The interior of St Petroc's Church showing the choir and chancel before the removal of the organ to the north, or farmers', transept in 1946. The choir stalls were made by Hems of Exeter and presented to the church in memory of George Cholmondeley of Glazebrook in 1926 and match the organ screen. The communion rails are part of the medieval rood-screen removed from the church in 1870. (CRANCH COLLECTION)

major change took place in the church. In 1946 the organ was moved from behind the choir stalls into the north transept and the area turned into a memorial chapel to commemorate those lost in the Second Word War. In 1947 Revd R.A. Edwards, the new rural dean, commented that 'the improvement in the appearance of the church is most marked.' His successor, Revd L.S. Ketchley, wrote in 1949 that, 'The Vicar and Church Council are to be congratulated upon the excellent way in which this church is cared for.'

In 1950 Revd A. Lawrence Vesey was inducted as vicar. One of the first tasks to take place in his incumbency was the re-nailing of the roof. In 1954 Mr William Knott, verger of the church for over 60 years, took the then rural dean, Revd W. Dove, around the church, as Revd Vesey was recovering from a motor accident which had occurred whilst he was on holiday. Revd Dove was also very complimentary about the state of the church in general.

The London Inn Excursion of 1933

During the mid-twentieth century many of the local events and happenings were the subject of poems written by Mr Albert Elliott. Here he describes the London Inn excursion of 22 July 1933.

You can talk of prohibition,
Of tea fights on the sands,
Of rambles round the moorlands,
Or hiking on the land;
But if you need a 'good old time',
With something with a 'push on',
Just pack your grip and take a trip
On the London Inn Excursion.

At 8-15 the signal fell!
We steamed out true to time!
'The Guard' himself quite satisfied
That barrel held just 9.
Not 99, as some had hoped,
For some are always craving
For an extra 'pint', but I advise
Salt water best for bathing.

Away we sailed to Slapton Sands,
Great crowds turned out to greet us;

The London Inn darts teams in the early 1950s. Left to right: *Tom Pyatt (the landlord), Eric Rush, Les Fox, Cecil Wilkinson, Jim Andrews, Mike Witheridge, George Chandler, Charlie Couchman and Alfie Andrews.*

(ALAN JONES COLLECTION)

Some thought that we were 'Nancy's pets',
Or Bertram Mills's circus;
But we were lads all out for fun,
Especially one 'Old Timer',
For 'Nobby' licked his lips and smiled
When he espied that 'niner'.

When the guard gave the word dismount,
We soon had empty buses.
One member of our party looked
Like Moses in the rushes.
Beef, Beer and Pasties soon were served
By faithful hands, and willing;
Some played a game of 'Pitch and Toss',
To earn a humble shilling.

Again we went at such a pace.
The drivers put fine work in;
For all the boys were anxious
To call on old George Turpin,
And there he was, the same old face,
Our hearts they missed a beat
As Theo's song brings memories back,
'Tis good when old friends meet.

Away once more across the Dart,
Where we almost came a cropper,
For No. 3 looked safely booked
For 'Davy Jones's Locker';
And when again we put to sea
A Dreadnought we should charter,
For Harry's weight, I understand,
Is sixteen and a quarter.

On, on again, like birds of flight
To Torquay, for our dinner;
If any felt dissatisfied
Then woe betide that sinner.
To pass remarks about the songs,

I ought not perhaps to do so,
But on his form 'Old Nimbo' would
Knock spots off Caruso.

At Haytor Rocks a halt was called,
The strain we all were feeling;
Some stood their ground like Britons,
While quite a few were kneeling.
The Band, of course, could be excused,
They lay amongst the heather,
With Theo and Arthur quite prepared
To do or die together.

In Plymouth, where we had our tea,
(You'll please excuse my laugh),
I saw some hair stand on its ends;
As if they felt the draught,
When up the lift we quickly flew,
A wash and brush up made,
'Old Tom' and 'Bun' seemed very pleased
With the mannequin parade.

Some of our boys, of course you know,
In 'Rags' are interested,
So 'Tom' and 'Joe', 'Alf' and 'Taff',
The 'models' soon inspected.
The prices were, I must admit,
A bit above our reach,
But the Old Firm can fix you up
At one and sixpence each.

Then 'Home, Sweet Home', the order came!
All hands on deck at 9,
We voted soundly that we would
All come again next time.
For when we parted on the shore –
With Mother's arms to rest on,
I think with me, you'll all agree,
It's due to Theo. Preston.

A late-1940s Brent football team, identified by Ken Creber. Left to right, back row: Alf Honeywell, Des Newman, Roy Tucker, Arthur Hill, Jim Andrews, 'Knobbler' Gordon Chapple; front row: 'Snaker' Joint, Maurice O'Connell, Wilf Honeywell, Trevor Budden, Vic Newman. (HONEYWILL COLLECTION)

A late-1940s South Brent football team. Left to right, back row: Fred Smallridge, Desmond Newman, Roy Tucker, Jim Andrews, Gordon 'Nobbler' Chapple, Edgar 'Eggie' Male and Cecil Wilkinson; front row: Clifford Joint, Royston Parsons, Eddie Sowden, Mossy O'Connell, Victor Newman. (WOOD COLLECTION)

A South Brent football team of the early-twentieth century. Taken by W.R. Gray, the photograph includes 'Curly' Bunker, Jack Ryder, Alf Manning, George Wilkinson, Ernie Catt senr, Reg Staples, Gordon and Lendle Wakeham, Bill Chapple, Jack Soper and Raymond Foale. (INEZ JORDAN collection)

A pre-First World War football team.

In 1984 the Pack Horse entered a team in the carnival cricket competition. They played on the cricket field at Hillside and were knocked out of the competition by the London Inn. Ben Wilkins scored 30 out of their 33 runs and the umpires were Peter Brown and Doug Petch. The team was, left to right, Larry Wootton, Peter Johnson, Jonathan Tubman, Ben Wilkins, David Newman, Bob Widdowson and Harry Jones. (WILKINS COLLECTION)

The Playing-field

The first playing-fields were situated on the field called Pool Park, which originally belonged to John Elliott, the lord of the manor. In 1888 it was sold to Mrs John Smerdon of Dartington by the trustees of the Elliott estate. In 1899 he in turn sold it to Mrs Elizabeth Maye, who left it to her two sons, John Maye of South Brent and Thomas Maye of Hampshire. When Mr R.H. Gill bought the land in 1928 he paid £350 for what was then a smaller acreage. On 25 March 1929 the Parish Council resolved to acquire Pool Park:

... for the purposes of a recreational field, and that application be made to the Ministry of Health for their sanction to the purchase of the field and to the borrowing of the necessary money.

In June 1929 the junction of the road at Sanderspool Cross was widened and the council became the owners of the land in November.

At that time the Feoffees were asked to give an annual grant towards the maintenance and equipment of the parochial playing-field. The previous tenant of the field, Mr E. W. Mead, who was entitled to a year's notice, was pleased to hand over the land but did note that it was not perhaps the best land. A sum of £29.19s.9d. had been raised from recent concerts held at the school. Mr Wyndham Hull made it known that:

the Feoffees Trustees were always anxious and willing to assist in any good and approved object within the strict terms of their trust and acknowledged by themselves to be such. Moreover, that as the Playing Field had been acquired by the Parish Council; the Council would deem it wise to provide for its regular upkeep. Nevertheless, that help from the Trustees in some way was not impossible.

As well as the playing-fields at Sanderspool Cross there were three fine tennis courts in the fields behind the new cemetery, banked up from ground level to ensure that each court was perfectly level.

A Little on the Feoffees

The Feoffees, consisting of the vicar of South Brent, two churchwardens and other worthy people of the parish have long been trustees and custodians of the parish lands. As such they met (and still do periodically) to distribute monies to various worthy causes. The trustees served very long terms of office and so became very familiar with the needs of the parishioners. For example, Mr W. Pearse served for 54 years and Mr A.W. Cranch for 44 years. One of the trustees at the time of writing, Mr Robert Savery, has served for 30 years.

One of the duties of the Feoffees has long been to distribute gifts to 'the necessitous poor' at Christmas. Records show that on 26 December 1918 the trustees met in the vestry and adjourned to the Anchor for the purpose of meeting tenants and collecting rents; that on 26 December 1919 'poor gifts were distributed at noon at the Church entrance' but it had been decided not to give tickets to other than the families 'entitled to receive them'. In that year the trustees adjourned to the Royal Oak to receive rents. Christmas tenants were met in the Anchor in 1921, while in 1927 the weather was particularly severe and snow had fallen to a depth of several feet, with drifts making roads impassable in several places. Details of the 1934 distribution, again on Boxing Day, are given:

The Trustees according to custom distributed Gifts to poor people as formerly arranged for by ticket – in four classes as follows –
10/- to 15 Aged, infirm and necessitous people.
6/- to 22 widows and labourers with young children.
5/- to 29 working poor people not so necessitous as above.
4/- to 31 desirous applicants as consolation gifts.

The distribution again passes off quietly and pleasantly – and adjournment to the Royal Oak Hotel to meet such tenants as may be present to pay rent due to date was made. The Christmas gift right up until more recent times were vouchers to be used in local shops.

In 1936 the custom of distributing Christmas gifts to the poor on Boxing Day was discontinued because:

... the Clerk has reported cases of impertinence and dictatorial attitude on the part of a few women applicants expressing dissatisfaction (and ingratitude) with the efforts of the Trustees in the Past and tending to 'bad form' on Boxing Day at the distribution of Gifts in the precincts of the parish Church.

The clerk was requested to distribute the gifts personally before Christmas to prevent such 'desecration' of the church. The vicar offered the Vicar's Hall at the bottom of Church Street for the collection of rents from 2p.m. onwards.

Changes in the national provision for welfare after the Second World War meant that in late 1946 the trustees felt that the lists for gifts would have to be revised in light of the new Health Acts. It was felt that warning of this should be given to the recipients and vicar Revd Ivor Jones offered the use of the parish magazine for this purpose.

Money would also be given for medical purposes, including the South Brent Nursing Association and the Prince of Wales's Hospital in Plymouth. On one occasion it was decided that 'a weakly boy be given a supply of malt and Cod Liver Oil Extract as ordered by the medical Attendant for six months.'

The row of cottages in Brent Mill, c.1907, before their gardens were taken to widen the road and make the pavement. (CRANCH COLLECTION)

Throughout the period, money was made available to help both male and female apprentices, always subject to reports of satisfactory progress being made. It is often noted that the trustees read such reports carefully.

The trustees also held property which would be let out to families. In 1945 the question of a vacant cottage in Brent Mill arose, the property having been requisitioned for homeless families by the local authority. Although the cottage had not been advertised, there had been several written applications for tenancy. The trustees provisionally accepted a tenant and agreed to approach the local authority to have the requisition notice withdrawn which, by March 1946, it was. Throughout the Feoffees' minute book there are references to improvements being made and tenancies changing.

The Birth of SBADS

Arthur Manning continued at the forefront of

'Someone was playing the violin' – a sequence showing Lulu Hawke and dancers. (INEZ JORDAN COLLECTION)

'theatricals' in Brent until 1934, when ill health forced him to retire and the South Brent Amateur Dramatic Society came onto the scene. Prior to that, however, Mrs Reynolds produced *Magic Midnight* with 22 young people involved including Mr Manning's niece Doris and his brother Charlie, described as a born comedian, a good singer and 'altogether the most outstanding member of the cast'.

Among the early productions were two by Eden Phillpotts, *The Farmer's Wife* and *Devonshire Cream*, the latter not without drama itself when the original producer, Revd Marshall, was taken ill and the production taken over by Mrs Hodson. The society's fortunes were not good, however, and it did not produce any more plays for several years.

It was during the war years that Mrs Georgina Lucy Hawke, known to everyone as 'Lulu', began to turn the fortunes of the dramatic element of Brent around. In the spring of 1943 she staged a play entitled *Ladies in Waiting* in aid of the RAF. Maggie Taylor writes:

The dynamic Lulu lost no time in getting the next show on the road and three months later the village was treated to Eden Phillpotts's Yellow Sands, *another play in the Devonshire dialect. A special performance was later given to the American forces in the area and we are told that they very much enjoyed the play, though how they managed to understand a word defies all explanation.*

Lulu's pet parrot, who played the part of another parrot, caused some concern as someone had taught him to swear, so that all the time he was on the stage, the whole production team was rigid with fear. Fortunately, the parrot behaved himself. Many new members took part, among them George Salter as the boozy and belligerent old reprobate Uncle Dick and Charles Tothill, who played the rampant socialist Joe Varwell. He was also responsible for the set. It changed from part of the beach, with crab-pots, rustic seat, nets, cottage and full-sized fishing boat, to an old-fashioned parlour stuffed to the eaves with bric-a-brac and furniture, including the inevitable piano. There were nearly 90 props involved!

Lulu's next production was The Ghost Train, *set in the shabby waiting-room of a country railway station. At one point in the play the off-stage ghost train is supposed to rush through the station at speed, belching a substantial amount of steam all over the waiting-room set. The trouble was that a way of producing sufficient steam could not be found, and as opening night drew ever closer, nerves grew ever more stretched.*

Then George Salter had a sudden brainwave, and come the next rehearsal, he walked into the hall with his goose tucked underneath his arm.

No one believed that the plan would work, but Mr Salter was sure that it would, so the goose was put to the test. George's wife Gladys remembered the incident

Dick Whittington, *1946, with Charles Tothill as the headmaster and his son, Barry, at the blackboard.* Seated, left to right, back row: *David Grigor, Mrs Shepherd, ?;* front row: *Owen Winzer, Joan Crispin, ?, Joyce Tucker.*

(INEZ JORDAN COLLECTION)

Exterior of St Dunstan's Catholic Church from the west.
(CARROLL COLLECTION)

'as if it was only last week'. The goose, she explained, was heated on an oil-stove placed behind a flat near the up-stage door, and a bucket of cold water was put beside it, along with a member of the stage crew. The ghost train sound effect was then started up and just when the noise was at its loudest, showing that the train had reached the station, the hot goose was drenched with the freezing cold water – and in through the door and all over the set billowed the steam in abundance.

George was Brent's tailor, and his 'goose' was the special iron he used to press his newly made garments. There had never been a more hectic year for drama group members than 1945. Come to that, it was rather hectic for everyone else as well.

Lulu Hawke was forced to give up working with the drama society due to illness after the production of the *Thirteenth Chair* in 1946 and the chairmanship of a

revived society was eventually taken over in 1948 by George Preston. Several very successful pantomimes were staged at this time. During the first half of the 1950s the society's performances were almost all plays, and one of them witnessed the stage debut of a future professional actor. Maggie Taylor continues:

In April 1951 twelve-year-old Michael Edwards was picked to play Bill in Dear Octopus *and a year later was chosen for the part of Dunsford Biggs in* Golden Harvest. *He then left the village, eventually grew up, did his National Service with the RAF, and afterwards signed on at the Central School of Speech and Drama where he changed his name to Michael Gaunt. Since then he has appeared in over two-hundred stage productions and a fair number of television plays, including 'Blake's Seven' and 'Lilli', in which he played Lord Randolph Churchill.*

Miss Joy Carnochan whose high standards prompted some excellent performances and whose productions were the first to be entered into competition, produced eight of the nine plays produced in the early 1950s.

St Dunstan's Catholic Church

To mark the 60th anniversary of the consecration of St Dunstan's Church in 1996, Mrs Pat Crosbie wrote a short account of its history. She comments:

This little history of St Dunstan's on the 60th

The Sleeping Beauty, 1949

Vera Rush (centre) *with* (clockwise from centre top) *Eileen Piper, Joy Lang, Margaret Hard, Ena Hawkins, Betty Knapman, and Margaret Passmore.*

(INEZ JORDAN COLLECTION)

Left to right: *Royston Parsons, Nano O'Connell, Margaret O'Shea, Peter Moore.*

(INEZ JORDAN COLLECTION AND PARSONS COLLECTION)

Charles Tothill putting the 'lid' on William Windeatt, watched by John Salter and Trevor Jones.

(INEZ JORDAN COLLECTION)

Some of the cast of The Sleeping Beauty, *including Clive Wood, Dennis Austin, Lesley Kidger, David Gove, Pat Luscombe, Barry Tothill. Mary Windeatt, Ruby Field, Margaret Newman, Barbara Joint, Desmond Karkeek and Ann Hayman.*

(WOOD COLLECTION)

Left: *George Salter as Mother Hubbard and Owen Winzer as Mrs Jack Spratt.*

(INEZ JORDAN COLLECTION)

Right: Left to right, back row: *Owen Winzer, George Salter, Trevor Jones,* front row: *John Salter and William Windeatt.*

(INEZ JORDAN COLLECTION)

Above: *Dorothea Hayman, Ruth Dodd, Jean Uren, Inez Smeeth, Joyce Hughes, Ann Watts, Pat Luscombe, Betty Newman, Ann Stewart, and Jennifer Truan, dressed in their fine costumes, admire the reawakened Beauty.*

(MILLER COLLECTION)

The cast of the 1949 production on stage at the 2001 production.

(WOOD COLLECTION)

The cast of the 1949 production of The Sleeping Beauty *with the cast of the 2001 production.*

(WOOD COLLECTION)

The interior of St Dunstan's Catholic Church.

(CARROLL COLLECTION)

Anniversary is written simply as I remember it.

This story of the church really begins in 1936. The first Mass was said on the first Sunday of Advent – 29 November – by Father John Stephan OSB in a hired hall at the Royal Oak Hotel. The attendance was so encouraging that a decision was made to establish a Catholic church in the village.

The land purchased for the project was part of the garden attached to the Old Manor House at the bottom of Church Street. The building was an old Army hut, bought for the most part with funds donated by the widow of Walter Moyle Sherer, who rose to the rank of first deputy inspector in the Indian police service. Many others gave generous donations. The solemn blessing and inauguration was performed by the Bishop of Plymouth and the Abbot of Buckfast, dedicating the church to St Dunstan, the Archbishop of Canterbury and former Abbot of Glastonbury on 14 September 1937. My father, Bob O' Shea, laid the foundation-stone and helped put up the hut which, although a temporary measure, still stands today.

The pews and altar rail came from other churches, as did the organ which is also still in use.

Father Benedict used to ride a bicycle from Buckfast Abbey to say Mass on Sundays and Holy Days. A house was built below the church for him but unfortunately he never became resident. The Carroll family moved in and Mrs Carroll became the sacristan, seeing to the priest's vestments. She also gave him breakfast after Mass. My mother used to clean the church and Mrs Stanton arranged the flowers.

There were very few Catholics in the area then, the Stanton family, the Carrolls and the O'Shea family and a few others whose names I cannot recall. I was only seven at the time. More Catholics gradually came into the area.

St Dunstan's Catholic Church.

In 1939 war was declared, bringing American and English soldiers, who marched to St Dunstan's and St Petroc's every Sunday from their Army camp at Crowder Park. Later prisoners of war were billeted at the camp. More Italian prisoners of war were housed at Syon Abbey. They painted our church in their own style and we had many visitors to admire their handiwork. The Stations of the Cross were painted by an artist who was staying with Mrs Stanton at Splatton House.

After the war things went back to normal and the congregation continued to grow to approximately seventy. In 1938 my sister Mary was the first of many to be baptised in the church, which is licensed for weddings, and many have departed this earth with a service conducted at our church.

We are still looked after by the Abbey Priests. After Father Benedict there was Father Aidan, followed by our present priest, Father Sebastian, who also plays the organ.

Duck Street

At various times in its history Church Street has been referred to as 'Duck Street' because of the ducks that could be found in it. Mrs Mary Bradford's father, Mr Bob O'Shea was the owner of two such ducks as reported below.

A report in the *South Devon Times*, kindly included with permission, describes the scene:

Their Daily Routine at South Brent

Darby is a handsome, fat, black and green drake, and Joan, his partner, a duck of sleek plumage. These two are a feature in everyday life in South Brent where they have been 'residents' for two years and they belong to Mr and Mrs O'Shea.

Two years ago Mr O'Shea was given two 'very wild' birds. Joan was the wilder and she had her wings clipped to stop her from getting away.

Mr O'Shea lives in a neat little cottage in the village, but he had no garden to keep the birds in so he took them to a field next to the church for which he is the caretaker. For eighteen months they lived in peaceful

Mrs Helena Moores, in the early 1940s, in the courtyard at the rear of her cottage at the bottom on Church Street. The courtyard served all of the cottages, demolished in the 1960s, which stood where Cedarholme and Stag's Head House (formerly Sunavon) now stand.

(MITCHELL COLLECTION)

seclusion in the field and meals were taken to them every day. This programme suited the pair admirably until the cold weather and heavy snowfalls of the early winter.

They waddle to warmth
The winter nights were far too cold for them, so one evening, just before feeding time they decided to waddle up the land and up the main street in the village to the master's cottage and spend the night in the warm kitchen. This became a new daily routine, and now they don't wait for their meals to be brought; they waddle up to the cottage three times a day to take it. At 8.30 a.m., 12.30 a.m. and 5.30 p.m. they are seen making their way to the cottage.

From the field they waddle under a gate and up the lane, Darby in front with Joan, following step for step. At the corner by the Police Station they turn slowly and cross the road at exactly the same spot every day and they even hold up the traffic.

Without a Quack
At a shallow dip in the kerbstones they climb on the pavement and proceed along the main street and turn

up a narrow lane and into the cottage where a good feed awaits them. They pass the dogs and the cats without so much as a quack or turn of the head. And the cats and dogs of South Brent merely eye them on their way.

Lunchtime lasts, generally, about ten minutes or a quarter of an hour and they retrace their steps (Darby always leading) to the field where they take a nap.

Mrs O'Shea told the *South Devon Times* that:

... they first started this new habit when the cold spell made them more hungry than usual. At first the villagers used to watch for them, but now they are just another part of ordinary life, taking everything in their stride.

The Second World War

At the time of the outbreak of the Second World War, Nancy van der Kiste was on holiday at Didworthy Bridge House, where she had spent many happy holidays. She recalls how:

On 1st September Dr Bettinson came panting and puffing down from the Sanatorium and told us that the Germans had started bombing Poland, and he thought we ought to cut our holiday short and return to Norfolk.

She then goes onto remember how the family spent the day in hurried packing and closing up the house before they set off back to their home.

During the war Brent was home to both Liverpool and Scottish regiments and to the 29th US Brigade. David Carroll remembers the spectacle of the Liverpool and Scottish soldiers marching down the length of Church Street in full dress uniform behind the pipe bands to go to Church Parade at 11 o'clock on Sunday mornings. The American forces did the same when they succeeded them at Kerries Road.

This was before the days of full racial integration in the United States and the black troops were segregated from their white compatriots, with the white troops stationed along Kerries Road, where Crowder Park has since been built, and the black troops billeted at Glazebrook. The two groups were allowed out of camp on alternate nights to avoid any fighting.

Many people can remember the troops travelling along Church Street in their light tanks and en route for exercises out on the moors armed with Bren guns.

Norman Perkins remembers Chenhall's Garage at Brooklands having one pump for the American soldiers. One night some Afro-American GIs arrived in a tank to fill up with fuel. Alan Perkins, Norman's father, told them that the pump was switched off but that if they went up to the camp someone would come down and turn it on. The GIs replied that because they were black, there was no way that that would happen. Anita Perkins fed the GIs eggs and bread, which they ate American style, all mashed

97

Wellington Square during the Second World War, with Mrs Marshall's shop on the left. Note the markings on the kerb, to make the corner visible in the blackout. Only the furthest cottage of the terrace on the right still exists, now as Stag's Head House. (VERA JORDAN AND PARSON COLLECTIONS)

together. When the tank started up next morning it caused the garage roof to shift, so that after the war it had to be replaced.

In another incident, during the potato shortage, a lorry passing Brooklands spilled its load onto the road, burying Alan Perkins up to his neck in potatoes and spilling the Redex, which was then mistaken for blood – luckily no actual blood was spilled.

Mrs Vera Jordan, Mrs Pat Crosbie, Mrs Margaret Eales and Mrs Mary Bradford also recall the ENSA

concerts at the Church Hall. The younger village girls were certainly not allowed in to see them, although they did manage to sneak in once the show had started. Margaret Catt remembers being held up to a window so that she could see what was going on inside. Ernie Catt and his friends went up to the camp to see the films shown to the GIs in the cookhouse. The relationship between the Brentonians and the Americans was very good, and at least one Brent girl, Lorna Catt, married a GI and made her

South Brent Home Guard, including Messrs Rowe, French, Moore, Heard, Walker, Hobbs, Rawlings, Garland, Smallridge, Stancombe, Hayman, Hard, Joint, Rogers, Hodge, Truan, Watts, Winzer, Tornberg, Lang, Staples, Preston, Sparkes, Shillabeer, Goss, Ellis, Northey, Honeywill, Clifton, Male and Hobbs. (MILLER COLLECTION)

The South Brent Girls Training Corps on parade, 1943.
(CROSBIE AND HAYMAN COLLECTIONS)

Army Cadets, c.1943. Ernie Catt joined when he was 13. They met in the drill hall in Plymouth Road for square-bashing, rifle-drill and similar activities. Under the command of Charles Tothill they would go off to camp at Braunton or Weymouth. Ernie also organised the social events – good times indeed. (CATT COLLECTION)

The war did not pass Brent by, as this photograph proves. Here are the members of the Girls Training Corps, which was under the leadership of Mrs Sheppeard. The girls learned such things as first aid and physical training. The photograph includes Rosemary Samways, Vera Pinhey, Eileen Piper, Mrs Sheppeard, Pauline Bishop. Margaret Passmore, Vera Joint, Pat O'Shea, Rita Pearman, Joy Lang, Betty Stanley, Brenda Miller and evacuee Sheila O'Neill. (VERA JORDAN COLLECTION)

home in the United States.

During the war South Brent was host to at least two groups of evacuees. Refugees from Plymouth would flee the city to avoid the bombing, and looked to Brentonians to take them in overnight. Mrs Barbara Field fled the Plymouth blitz to stay with her Aunt, Mrs Lil Chandler, first in Corn Park and then in a cottage at Lutton. She recalls being in Plymouth during the blitz of 1941 and spending time in the Anderson Shelter, and remembers the relief felt by herself and her family when the all-clear was given after a raid. Barbara also recalls that the Misses Ward had two evacuees at Lutton House, where she had the job of cleaning the grates at 7a.m. before going to

school. Many Plymouth evacuees only stayed overnight, choosing to return to the city during the day. Mrs Barbara Lodge remembers that many of her relations came to stay with them at The Rock. She also recalls a lady doctor from Guernsey, who, just before the invasion of the Channel Islands, came to visit her daughters, who were at school in England, only to find herself stranded. She had no contact with her husband, also a doctor, for the duration of the occupation.

There were also evacuees from Eltham and Acton, in London. Mrs Margaret Eales, Mrs Mary Bradford, Mrs Pat Crosbie and Mrs Vera Jordan recall that the girl evacuees were not used to the range and variety of vegetables they were served even though it was wartime. Mr Jack Preston was the billeting officer responsible for housing evacuees and Mr O'Shea was his deputy. The Brent girls built up friendships with the evacuees, who knew much more about life and the ways of the world than themselves.

Rationing was a harsh fact of life, and cooking fat, butter and sugar were in short supply. Ernie Catt calls to mind the windfall that occurred when the Americans left Brent and dumped all their unused food supplies behind Quarry Park. Brentonians retrieved tins of fruit, cheese and many other unavailable goodies to supplement their wartime rations. Ernie also recollects there being a rumour that the Americans had dumped four jeeps still in kit form, but these were never found.

In 1939 the bell-ringers decided to suspend their

Chenhall's Garage first started business in the 1920s when there were very few cars about, most of them owned by the people who lived in the large houses. The original buildings were converted by Mr Chenhall from a farm, as the photograph shows. In the early years most of the income was from installing electricity in houses throughout the South Hams. After the Chenhall ownership it belonged for a short time to Mr Turner and was then taken over by Alan Perkins. Mr Perkins remained at the garage until his retirement in 1960, when it was bought by the Regent Oil Co. There were plans at the time to run the dual carriageway along the route of the A38, necessitating the demolition of both the garage and the London Inn and their relocation elsewhere. Regent pulled out when the route was changed and the garage became part of the Sopers Group, the Chenhall name moving to Collaton St Mary. The photograph inset shows the garage in its later Regent livery. The showroom, with Morris/BMC cars, was once a barn.

(PERKINS AND SPARKES COLLECTIONS)

weekly fees as the bells could not be rung during wartime. There is no record of an annual meeting being held until November 1944.

Mr A.J. Sparkes was appointed to the headship of South Brent Primary School in August 1939 and so was head teacher at the outbreak of the Second World War, a post he occupied for 29 years until his retirement in July 1968, making him the longest-serving Brent head teacher to date.

The purchase of capes for the use of children living some distance from the school became an issue at the outbreak of the Second World War.

The evacuees and their teachers joined the Brent children at school, with lessons alternating between mornings and afternoons on a weekly basis. Not only did they use the school, but also the Church Hall (which was divided in two by a curtain down the middle) and the Congregational and Methodist schoolrooms. Evacuee teachers included Mr Bunting (the headmaster), Mrs Spellamy and Miss Hobday, who are remembered as being very strict, and Miss Easton.

During the war Mr Sparkes wrote to the Brent Feoffees pointing out an interesting situation that had arisen. The minute book records that:

A letter from the Headmaster of the Council School was read pointing out that there were now some 140 locals and just over 200 evacuees in the school and that it was often found that some of the evacuees, for work, behaviour and attendance were more worthy of prizes than the local children and suggesting that consideration might be given to an additional grant for children who have been at this school for 12 months. The Headmaster also enquired whether, now that a canteen had been started, some help might be given to the children of needy families to purchase their dinners at school.

It was resolved that in addition to the usual grant of £5 for prizes, a special grant of £3 be made for evacuees, as suggested but that no allowance be made against dinners at school.

The people of South Brent, being so close to Plymouth, were very aware of what was happening to the city during the blitz years. Whereas today there is the orange glow of the city's sodium lights beyond Ugborough Beacon, during the blitz years the glow was from burning oil tanks which, once alight, burned for days. Brentonians could also hear the bombing, and children, although not really knowing what was going on, were frightened by the noise. At the height of the Plymouth blitz Mrs Barbara Lodge recalls standing in the garden of her home at The Rock drinking a cup of tea and watching with horror the orange sky beyond Ugborough. The next day she

Top and above: *Staff of the Army & Navy Stores including* (top) *Ken Miller, Frank Underhill and other men from Plymouth.* Above, left to right, back row: *Barbara Sleep, Joyce Tucker, Phyllis Moore, ?;* front row: *Gwennie May, Miss Collins, Joan Hard. The top picture also includes Ken Miller and Frank Underhill, along with other men from Plymouth.* (EALES COLLECTION)

went into Plymouth with an evacuee from the city who was staying at Craigmoor and drove around the ruined city in a bus to see just how dreadful it was. Margaret Catt recalls that when aircraft passed overhead on their way to Plymouth her father, who was in the Observer Corps, would take Margaret and her mother up the lane, away from their cottage in Noland Park. The aircraft, to her, were 'black things overhead making a noise'. She remembers hearing the impact of the bombs and the sound of gunfire as

attempts were made to bring the aircraft down. The family would not go back into the house until it was quiet, just in case bombs were dumped over Brent. Margaret also remembers that every time they went out her mother took a bag containing all the family papers, insurance documents and the like.

On one occasion a German aircraft crashed at Yalland Runs. Ken Fox recalls hearing a loud explosion at 6.30p.m. Villagers, including Ernie Catt, ventured out to see the wreckage. He remembers the two airmen who had bailed out of the twin-engined aircraft being killed by flying debris; he also remembers retrieving a Mae West flotation device which he found near the site. Mrs Barbara Lodge recalls the French governess to the children at Yonder Cross trying to get close to the wreckage but being held back by the men guarding it. People also tell of dogfights that took place in the skies over the village.

One memory of the war years was of air-raid practices. Mrs Pat Crosbie remembers having to go out into the fields where Courtenay Park now stands to practise lying down. Drills in school involved the children crawling under their desks – although they successfully got their heads safely tucked in, their bottoms were invariably left sticking out!

The vicar, Revd Gallagher, was responsible for sounding the alert by blowing a whistle in the street. On one occasion a Co-op employee en route from Buckfastleigh to Brent saw a parachutist coming down. The Revd Gallagher came out into the street with his shotgun whilst everybody else stayed indoors. Pat Crosbie recalls there being a raid as she took seven children for a walk around Aish one Sunday afternoon – they hid under a hedge for two hours before venturing home.

Mrs Barbara Lodge remembers keeping watch for parachutists from the top of Brent Hill, she and her sister-in-law, an evacuee, sitting back to back so that they could see across the whole of the moors. She also recalls the upright poles placed on open moorland to prevent enemy aircraft from landing. Watching for parachutists was no easy task – Ken Fox remembers the alarm once being raised when a Brentonian saw what he thought were parachutists over Ugborough Beacon – it was only a trick of the failing light caused by the setting moon.

Although there was never a direct hit on Brent, Pat Crosbie recalls the time when three bombs were ditched over Shipley after a raid on Plymouth. She remembers that the explosion caused the wallpaper on the ceiling of their Church Street cottage to come down. When they realised it was only the paper that had come down rather than the whole ceiling, they had to fight their way out of it pantomime-style.

The men of the Home Guard stood watch at Marley Tunnel to prevent sabotage and to carrry out fire-watch on the moor. So that they could find their way home in the dark, an arrangement was made for a passing train to open its fire-box as it crossed the Glazebrook viaduct to give the men an indication of which was the way home. One result of the blackout seems to have been that children would bump into familiar things in the dark.

Margaret Eales has particular memories of the Army & Navy Stores, which were in the outbuildings of what is now the Church House. The stores, selling groceries and provisions, had been blitzed out of Plymouth and remained in Brent for four years, all that time making deliveries to Mrs Bastard at Kitley House and to the Earl of Morley at Saltram. There was also a chemist and a tobacconist and confectioners. Of course local people could also register their coupons at the Co-op and at Tidballs, and there are memories of queuing for bananas.

Brent was also temporary home to German and Italian prisoners of war, who worked on local farms. They were treated in a very relaxed way, and even played football for Brent.

The Women's Institute also played its part in the war effort:

Members went to a Military Hospital Supply Depot each week to take home knitting and needlework. Sugar given by special grant enabled members to make two hundred and ten pounds of blackberry and apple jam in September 1941.

From May to September foxgloves grow in profusion in Brent's lanes, so:

From as early as the 1930s, the leaves and seeds from this valuable plant were collected and sent to Newton Abbot for processing into digitalis, a drug required for treating, amongst other ailments, heart disease. Combined with the W.V.S. and local schoolchildren, members helped to collect 200 tons of fresh leaves. In

one year it is recorded that seeds weighing one pound 13 ounces resulted in the WI being paid the princely sum of seven shillings and fourpence.

Used stamps were saved and collected by members. In 1942, 8,750 were sent to Hackney Children's Hospital and in 1944 a further 12,000 stamps were sent to add to the fund.

The WI hut was let to evacuees in 1941 and the WI held meetings in a number of different places for the next three years.

David Carroll remembers there being a small German prisoner-of-war camp at Syon Abbey, one of the prisoners from which stayed on in England after the war, got married and worked on a local farm.

During the war, a Brentonian stationed in India wrote this poem about his native county:

This conflict has taken us far apart
As from place to place we roam,
But nothing here thrills my heart
Like the Countryside at home.

Those Devon streams with banks of green,
The roaring of the falls.
Those daffodils they droop and dream
When Spring with its beauty calls.

The Summer and the lovely days
In Devon's winding lanes.
The cunning hovering of the Hawk
Waiting for their prey.

The moors with their heathered cloak
Rise against the sky.
The staunchness of the giant oak
'Till Autumn takes its pride.

These beauties are but just a few
Of the Country in our Devon.
The only place I really know
Which I could call my heaven.

When this struggle comes too close
My home town waits for me.
'Till then my heart will send its song
And pride 'till we are free.

The War Agricultural Committee ordered the ploughing of land including the Feoffees' land known as Haydons, as well as other holdings. When an order was served on the tenant of Haydons requiring him to plough five of his six fields, the clerk to the Feoffees was instructed to lodge an appeal against it – noted at the next meeting as having been received. Similarly in 1941, when No. 1 Feoffee Cottages became vacant and was requisitioned for war use, 'The trustees accepted the position'.

In August 1940 assistance was given by the

Among those watching this VE Day procession are Arthur Parsons, Colin Shillabeer, Rose Karkeek and Jimmy Garland.

Waiting outside the Anchor for the VE Day carnival procession. (Wood Collection)

trustees for the cleaning, lighting and heating of a room for WEA lectures, but it was agreed 'the people attending were considered well–off enough to pay for their own accommodation and in future such help was to be discontinued.' There was also a request for classes to study for Air Force qualification. The trustees considered that, 'in the light and report of its usefulness in Brent' the matter should 'lie' on the table. In the end only one student came forward.

In 1942 John Eales started a Sunday paper round

South Brent marked the Allied victory in 1945 with many events, including this street party in Wellington Square on 8 May. In a carnival atmosphere, there were decorations in abundance all over town. (Wood Collection)

in Rattery with papers that he bought from Miss Manning's newsagent's in Brent. He recalls Miss Manning at work in her shop assisted by her aunt who, though blind, never made a mistake at the till. He also recalls the daily papers, on arriving at Brent Station in sack trucks, being trundled down to the shop by porter Jack Garland. When troops assembled at Marley Head for the D Day landings John needed a special permit to get from Rattery to Brent.

The War Ends

Victory was declared in Europe in 1945 and Mr O'Shea rang the Toll House bell with an enamel pan on his head in case the stones fell on him. There was a bonfire in the square and Mary Bradford, wrapped in an army coat, was brought by a lodger to watch it.

Maggie Taylor writes of the celebrations at the end of the Second World War:

The bells were ringing to announce the arrival of VE Day, and the whole village was suddenly flung into a frantic whirl of activity. Flags and bunting were hastily hoisted, festive events were rapidly arranged, mainly by the drama group's Trevor Jones, red, white and blue clothing was quickly made, and every last table and chair in Brent was hauled out and placed along the length of Church Street, ready for the children's tea party.

Food was still on ration of course, but nevertheless there was a right royal spread – or so it must have seemed to the hordes of youngsters who sat at the tables stuffing themselves with fish paste sandwiches, red and yellow jellies, powdered lemonade made up into a drink, and South Brent's own traditional tuff cakes (soft bread rolls spread with jam and cream, for those who don't already know). Arthur Manning brought out his harmonium and played popular songs for the little diners, who somehow managed to sing along without ceasing to eat.

After the meal, the tables were removed to make way for a Floral Dance all round the village, which was followed by a trek to the top of Brent Hill to witness the

The VE Day celebrations. The photograph includes: *Miss Greenaway, George Hill, Henry Stone, Christine Preston, Dolores Trundle, Ena Hawkins, Vilma Trebble (Queen) Pauline Bishop June Andrews, George Trundle, Mickey Salter, Pat Salter and Nano O'Connell.* (PARSONS COLLECTION)

lighting of a mammoth bonfire and to generally lark around until it was time to watch the fireworks display. Back in Wellington Square, Arthur Manning was on again, playing the music for the dancing and singing that went on until nearly dawn.

Next day there was a party for the senior villagers, arranged by Carmen Manning, and for the children there were sports and games in the field opposite the school. That evening saw the Church Hall festooned in decorations of red, white and blue, for the occasion of the Grand Victory Ball, music by Arthur's dance band.

Two days later it was Carnival time. Alice Vickery crowned the Victory Queen and Nano O'Connell won a prize in the fancy dress parade.

Sunday dawned with another parade, in which every uniformed body in the place, right down to the teeniest Brownie, marched behind the band to St Petroc's Church for a special thanksgiving service. But they hadn't finished yet because as well as all that there were two concerts, another dance and another fancy-dress parade. Another Brentonian said: 'We'd never had so much to do in Brent. There was something going

The 1945 grand concert to celebrate the end of the war. Amongst the cast are producer Lulu Hawke (centre) and co-producer Betty Sheppeard, with George Salter, Eileen Piper, Edward Rowe, Ena Hawkins, Gwen Joint, Violet Manning, Christine Preston, Vera Pinhey, Mary Sparkes, Vera Karkeek, Joan Crispin, Margaret Winzer, Pauline Bishop, Marjorie Hard, Eileen May, Owen Winzer (in dark glasses) with Irvy Wood and other members of Mr Manning's dance band.
(INEZ JORDAN, WOOD AND MEAD COLLECTIONS)

'We'll hang out our washing on the Siegfried line', from the 1945 concert. Left to right: *Eileen May, Vera Karkeek, Joan Crispin, Ena Hawkins, Pauline Bishop, Eileen Piper, Mary Sparkes, ?, Vera Pinhey.* (INEZ JORDAN COLLECTION)

'Daisy Belle', a sketch featuring (left to right) *George Salter, Lulu Hawke, Mr Edgcumbe and Gladys Hannaford.* (INEZ JORDAN COLLECTION)

A night at the ballet – the swan and two ugly sisters. Left to right: *Owen Winzer, Dorothy Sheppeard, Francis 'Punchy' Manning.* (INEZ JORDAN COLLECTION)

on morning, noon and night and some of us, the young ones, didn't get to bed 'till it was time to get up again.'

For Anita and Alan Perkins, though, there was one tiny flaw amid all this joy. They had been given a large bottle of good Champagne, to be consumed on VE night, and it was duly uncorked and one drink each poured out for the Perkins and their lodger. At which moment a tumult outside announced the arrival of a troupe of revellers, who were doing the Conga up Plymouth Road and singing at the tops of their voices. So Anita and Alan decided to go and join in the fun for a while. But they got so caught up in it all that they forgot to come back in. Eventually, though, the troupe danced off and the two Perkins returned indoors, all ready for an evening of bubbly drinking – only to find the Champagne bottle with not a drop left in it and their lodger lying flat on her back in a deep and happy sleep!

The week-long celebrations were rounded off by a very successful production of the anonymous letters mystery *Poison Pen*, though it was not for its success that Marjorie Skinner would always remember it.

Brent Celebrates

Above: *The Royal Oak*; centre: *Totnes Road*; right: *Clifton Terrace, all decorated for Hospital Week, 1913.*
(ANDERSON AND CRANCH COLLECTIONS)

Fore Street, South Brent. Note the Pratt's Petrol sign at the corner of Stockbridge Lane next to Wakeham's. The cottages with the lower roofs on the left- hand side of Church Street are on the site where the Co-op was later constructed. (ANDERSON COLLECTION)

The WI cake stall on 8 May 1993, when South Brent held a Victorian Fun Day. Left to right, back row: Betty Skinner, Caroline Bland, Wendy Woodley, Doreen Puddefoot, Pauline Juste, Rosemary Evans; front row: Esther Warnes, Joy Hayman, Sylvia Warman, Win O'Connor, Vera Bennett, Stella Stickland.
(WI COLLECTION)

The Victorian Spectacle, May 1993.
(HAYMAN COLLECTION)

David Gove, Bunty Mortimore and Des Karkeek setting off for Penhale, near Newquay in Cornwall, in 1950.

(KARKEEK COLLECTION)

Marjorie, who played the part of Rose Rainrider, got married half-way through the production to Lieut Jack Vaira of the United States Army – and then postponed the honeymoon they'd planned so that the play could finish its run. Later in the year she went off to America, there to raise a family. In the 1950s when she returned for a long holiday, she re-joined SBADS, served on the committee and took part in three more plays.

With two productions in around four weeks the Players must have thought that they were due for a rest. There wasn't the slightest chance; even as Poison Pen *was packing 'em in, Lulu and Betty Sheppeard were devising a show to mark the end of the war in Europe – and what a show it turned out to be.*

A joint effort of the Players and the village, the Victory Variety Concert, as it came to be known, went on stage in the following July and was one almighty smash hit. Three one-act plays started it off and then came the main event, a lavish and colourful extravaganza which had the title Dancing Through the Ages.

A veritable cornucopia of entertainment, it opened with the hit songs of the recent war, then rolled back through history with exhibition dances of the 1920s, Edwardian drawing-room ballads, items from the Victorian music hall, nautical scenes from the days of Lord Nelson, a selection of dances from the early days of ballet, songs and stories in a medieval turret, and a host of other historical scenarios, ending up with a large set-piece in which Bronze Age Brentonians welcomed home their warriors returning from battle.

The whole show was beautifully costumed too, a wondrous achievement in those days of clothing coupons and the dire shortage of materials. Without doubt the most successful and popular production that

had ever been staged in the village, it played for three nights to a Church Hall packed to overflowing, and still Alice Vickery, in charge of the seating, was being pestered for tickets. The company, therefore, gave another performance, which also played to a packed Church Hall, and when the final totting-up came to be done, it was found that almost 1,500 people had paid to see the show – a record that remains unbroken.

August brought an end to the war with Japan and another week of jollifications for Brent, with Wellington Square flood-lit for the occasion by John Hawke, Lulu's son and the Players' electrics man. There was no big production this time though. Instead, the Players took part in a concert arranged by the local Royal Marines, and a month later, by special request, they resurrected Poison Pen *and took it to Totnes to help raise money for the town's Welcome Home fund.*

Two Memorable Years

Des Karkeek did his National Service in the years immediately after the Second World War. He recalls his experiences as 22475360 CFN Karkeek.

Just after his eighteenth birthday Des was called up into the army, which was not his first choice. He was posted to REME camp at Honiton for basic training, which he describes as 'six weeks of hell'. His years in the Army Cadet Force helped. Training over, he was posted to Ellesmere.

At Ellesmere, it was back to the classroom to learn the theory of administering TLC to heavy army lorries which were ageing in that they had already survived the war. Having passed the various tests, a few short postings followed. One to a camp in Feltham in Middlesex, now the renowned dwelling place for some of the most unfortunate young offenders.

Eventually I joined the 6th Transport Company RASC. Thirteen REME were supposed to keep over 100 assorted vehicles maintained and roadworthy. In convoy we often carried The Duke of Cornwall Light Infantry (DCLI). We were stationed near Swindon for a few weeks and I often crept out and hitched a lift home for a couple of days. We were awaiting sea transport from Southampton, to take the trucks to Holland. One of my buddies was a Dick Pearce, who was permitted to disappear on a Friday evening, to reappear on Sunday. He was a well-known Everton player; pro-footballers used to enjoy these privileges.

Des was next posted to north-west Germany, not far from the Iron Curtain.

For over a year we spent most of our time following convoys of wagons. Having a motorcycle licence, I had to take my turn to ride up and down the convoy trying to keep everyone on the same road after crossroads, traffic lights and railway crossings. It was one of the most dangerous jobs in National Service. Many roads were cobbled and when it was wet, were deadly to ride a bike on.

One of Des's pleasures has been music and while based in Germany he was able to go to concerts both in London and in some German cities – he still has his ticket for the Vienna Philharmonic in Munster.

Most of my leisure time was taken up with soccer since four of our thirteen REME lads were professional players. Tradition in the Army was that the officers played rugger, the sergeants played hockey and the men soccer. There were a few exceptions. One of our officers was a brilliant soccer player and pulled a shirt on with the lads.

Our officers progressed to the semi-final of a British Army of the Rhine rugger tournament. There was only one non-officer in the side; a lad called Davis who played for Teignmouth and Devon. He knew that I had played rugger at King Edward VI School and thus it was that when they had a number of injuries I found myself lining up in the BAOR semi-final and final. We were 15 points up at half-time and scraped home by one point.

After soccer we would be lucky to get tea in the cook house. But, after the rugger match came an unforgettable experience. We played at Baden Baden. After the match we dined in a huge banqueting hall which had been the property of the Krup families and was untouched by the war. The banqueting hall was oval and had a 'gallery' with a large number of busts of the best-known composers, writers and artists.

The pay of a National Service man was very low. I did, however, discover one or two ways of making an extra pound (Marks actually). I was fortunate not to

Ken Fox, some time between the wars with two Dartmoor otter hounds at the gates of the vicarage. (FOX COLLECTION)

smoke but I somehow obtained an extra cigarette ration card. The cigarettes were easily sold for about three times the buying price to the Germans. We also sold the odd four-gallon can of petrol when we were on manoeuvres, often to farmers.

Des found his experience of National Service a good one and he made a number of real friends. His footballing brought privileges not enjoyed by all and he had a few strokes of luck, not least of which was avoiding being posted to some of the more dangerous parts of the globe, such as Korea.

Social Activities

Country Pursuits

Rabbiting was an activity in which many people took part. Ken Fox maintains that the rabbits on the moor were the best. He recalls going out with the vicar's son, Charles Gallagher, and catching as many as 60 rabbits in a day. Mongrel dogs were the best to take rabbiting and Ken remembers Jock Lang's dog, a spaniel–whippet cross, as being one of the finest. Boxing Day was a big rabbiting day – they would watch the Dartmoor Hunt meet in the village in the morning in Fore Street and go rabbiting in the afternoon. The members of the rabbiting fraternity could tell when rabbits were about, even if they could not be seen. Ken remembers going out with his father.

He told me that there was a rabbit in a certain burrow. When I asked him how he knew he told me to look at the grass which was lying towards the burrow which told him the rabbit was in there. If the burrow was empty the grass would be lying the other way.

Revd Gallagher kept polecats to control the rats in hayricks. The rick would be surrounded with wire netting and the polecats sent in. As the rats emerged they would be killed by men waiting on the outside of the netting.

Out on the Town

The young men of the village would often go off to Buckfastleigh for a night out, taking the 4.20p.m. bus from the London Inn. In Buckfastleigh they would go to Mrs Crannaford's café for a cup of tea before going to the pictures. On one occasion, one of the boys pocketed some café buns for later. After the pictures, they went off to a dance at the town hall only to find, when they came out, that it was pouring with rain. The queue for taxis was so long that it was decided to walk back to Brent. In the early hours they stopped off to rest in a barn, where one of the lads, striking a match to see around him, was reminded in no uncertain terms of the risk of fire. At dawn, as they set off to finish the journey, one of the boys claimed he could eat a horse and its rider.

Country Pursuits

The Hunt in Station Road in the late-nineteenth century. The Dartmoor Hunt has traditionally met in South Brent each year on Boxing Day. No. 1 Station Road was built where the railings are, on the right of the photograph. (MILLER COLLECTION)

Beating of the Outer Bounds at Western Whitaburrow, 1910. (CRANCH COLLECTION)

Crowds gather outside the Post Office at Brent Fair, 1919. Note the pony in the foreground. (ANDERSON COLLECTION)

Mr Jack Luce hay harvesting at Lower Downstow in the 1960s. (ANDERSON COLLECTION)

Brent gymkhana in the 1920s. (INEZ JORDAN COLLECTION)

Haymaking out at the crossroads, 1945, with (left to right): *Margaret O'Shea, June Andrews, Clifford Bishop, and Nano O'Connell, with John Wild* (front). (WOOD AND WILD COLLECTION)

Carnival Fun and Games

Carnival 1930s style.
(ANDERSON COLLECTION)

The carnival in 1951 – South Brent Dance Club's entry was 'National Butter' and the girls were dressed all in yellow.
(INEZ JORDAN COLLECTION)

Carnival day, 28 June 1957. Getting ready for the off on the Co-op float are (left to right) Margaret O'Shea, Brenda Newman, Nano O'Connell, Jim Andrews and Bill Maddock. (WOOD COLLECTION)

Peter and Jean Miller, all dressed up and ready to go collecting at Brent carnival in 1976.
(MILLER COLLECTION)

Mr Wild's milk delivery van outside The Leaze. The van was decorated for the carnival at the time of the Persian oil crisis. John Wild senr is Old Father Time and with him are Vic Poulton and John Wild junr and Monty the dog, who always sat in the middle of the road outside his Wellington House home when the church bells rang.
(WILD COLLECTION)

Brent Bands

South Brent Band Week, August 1926. On the far left, dressed as a pierrot, is band leader Mr Arthur Manning.   (ANDERSON COLLECTION)

John van der Kiste, Peter Lewis, Alan Davis and Peter Bovey performing live at the Royal Oak on 21 May 1978.
(VAN DER KISTE COLLECTION)

Brent Band in the 1930s. Left to right, back row: Fred Smallridge, ?, Theo Preston, Arthur Manning, Charles Lang, Dudley Owen, William Pinhey, Norman Hard; front row: Gordon Wakeham, Ernie Catt senr, Raymond Foale, Mr Vooght, Charlie Manning junr.

(ANDERSON COLLECTION)

South Brent Mothers' Union

The South Brent Mothers' Union, which was founded in 1902, at a garden party in the grounds of Whinfield in the early 1930s. Sitting in the centre is Mrs Anne Collier, the enrolling member.

(INEZ JORDAN COLLECTION)

Three ladies and a vicar, April 1989. St Petroc's Church has always been noted for its cleanliness, and here we have one of the teams responsible – Eirlys Prickett, Audrey Pawson with her daughter Sally and Beth Merriman (who was behind the camera). The vicar is Revd David Niblett.

In March 2002 the South Brent Mothers' Union celebrated its centenary. Here members and their guests from across the deanery and diocese enjoy the tea held after the 100th Anniversary service in St Petroc's Church. Inset: The centenary cake.

(MOTHERS' UNION COLLECTION)

Members of the South Brent Mothers' Union at a carnival street fair. Left to right: Eunice Vallance, Nancy Wright, Lillian Wakeley and Sheila Wall.

South Brent Primary School infants, 1957.

(TIDBALL COLLECTION)

South Brent Primary School, early 1950s.

(MITCHELL COLLECTION)

A.W. Cranch outside his shop. (CRANCH COLLECTION)

Reaching into his pocket for the buns he had saved the previous day, the lad found nothing but a pocketful of crumbs – a rat had eaten the buns while he slept.

The young men had their own song, as recalled by Bert Field:

We are the South Brent boys.
We never make no noise.
We know our manners,
How to spend our tanners,
We are respected wherever we go,
As we go walking down South Brent streets
Doors and windows open wide,
Here the South Brent boys are out.
Hear the South Brent boys all shout,
'We are the South Brent boys!'

On another occasion, one New Year's Eve, a group had been to a dance in Totnes. When they came to leave there was no hope of getting a taxi back to Brent so they decided to walk to Totnes Station, where they slept in a milk lorry. In the early hours of the

morning they began to walk home and were picked up by a Post Office van, all piling in on top of the postbags. When they got to Palston Bottoms the van's radiator cap blew from carrying so much weight, at which point its passengers got out and walked, leaving the van stranded.

The Good Work Continues

The ladies of Brent continued to attend meetings of the WI and Mothers' Union. In 1948, at a demonstration by members of hairdressers Richard Henry of London and Rome on how to manage one's hair (their models wore the latest hairstyles), two WI members were invited to have their hair styled during what must have been an enlightening afternoon! In the winter of 1948 the WI was asked by the Food Executive Office to help Mrs Brockington at the village chemist with the distribution of vitamins. For this purpose, the WI hut was opened on the first and third Tuesday of every month, though in the following year the operation was moved to Mrs Briggs's house behind Church Street, as the hut was too far for some mothers to go. After the war, the always-popular jumble sales were often held to raise funds, left-over items being sent to St Peter's Clergy House at London Dock for distribution to the poor. In the 1952 flooding disaster which hit Lynton and Lynmouth and members agreed to donate five guineas to the WI fund for distressed members. Mrs Vickery opened a clothing depot for the flood areas and 215 articles were sent, including blankets and five men's suits.

The Village Postman

Bert Field remembers his postman's round in the mid-twentieth century in great detail. He would be up at 4.30a.m. in order to sort the mail by 5.30a.m. His deliveries would begin with the Anchor Hotel, from where he would deliver to Hillside and up as far as the Colliers at Whinfield. He then came back to deliver along 'Harry Waters Lane' (Harwell Lane) and thence to Inglenook and Forder. Next, he would

113

Mr Alfred Hard, seen here on Nancy, was granted leave to ride a pony to deliver the post as he was responsible for a country round, delivering mail to outlying farms twice a day. Some of those still living in Brent in 2005 remember him delivering special letters on Nancy.

The original George V postbox at the Post Office.

Below: *Fore Street, c.1920, with the jubilee lamp in place, before the Co-op was built.* (PANNELL COLLECTION)

South Brent Post Office, 2000.

High jinks in the square, 1968: Grant Ford and Michael Male climb onto the jubilee lamppost. (GRANT FORD COLLECTION)

cross the fields to deliver at Yonder Cross before returning to Harbourneford, where he would clear the telephone box of cash once a month. His round then took him over the top fields to Stippadon, and at Gisperdown he would have breakfast. He would then leave his bike outside the gate and walk over to Dockwell. After delivering to the hamlet of Lutton, Bert would finally return to the office by about 10.30a.m. In the spring, delivery might contain 14lb bags of turnip seed and if there was a telegram to be delivered when he got back, he would be off again.

The afternoon shift started at 2.15p.m. with a bit of sorting and then the first delivery to the waterboard house on Exeter Road. The route then took Bert to Stidston, Rattery Mill over the dangerous bridge along Culver Lane and then down into Rattery village. From here, it went to Syon Abbey (where there would often be tea and biscuits) via Knowles Farm. The Abbey was a closed order – indeed it is the only such English community to have survived intact since it was founded in 1415 – and once Bert had rung the bell a heavy bolt would be pulled back and the mail placed in a revolving drum behind a grille. The return journey to Brent was via Stidston. Mail was then sorted and taken up to the station for 7.30p.m to catch the mail train. If the train was late, Bert had to wait to make sure the guard signed for the bag.

CHAPTER 7

The Turner Era, 1954–78

The Anchor corner showing the construction of the Co-op, 1925/26.

1950s – a Busy Place To Be...

Brent was a self-sufficient place in the middle of the twentieth century. The Brent branch of the Buckfastleigh Co-operative Society was in effect a small department store where you could get anything. Margaret Catt remembers working there from the time she was 18. Going through the front door you found the grocery department. Colin Shillabeer had a counter to the left where he was responsible for cheese, bacon and butter – the forerunner of the delicatessen. The range of cheeses was not great at this time, Cheddar, Gorgonzola and perhaps Edam. Margaret recalls the girls' horror when a Gorgonzola cheese was cut open and found to be alive with maggots! Monday was weighing-up day, when all the loose goods, such as dried fruit, sugar, spices, pepper, etc., were put into blue bags ready for sale. Arthur Parsons was a dab hand at twisting cones for the smaller quantities. There was a store room at the back for weighing up larger items, including potatoes and, at the right time of the year, seed potatoes such as 'Home Guard', chicken feed, maize etc. Outside was a tank for paraffin. Margaret

remembers having to wash her hands after she served it before going back into the grocery. A staircase ran up the centre of the store and the cashier had a little office underneath at the back. The assistants would send the customer's money in a container, operated by a pulley system, to the cashier, who would then send it back with the change. On the

Relaxing in-store at the Co-op Christmas party, 1985. Left to right: Jean Miller, Pauline Richards, Margaret Catt, ?, Kenny Lyne, Anya Cockings, Joy Hayman, Amanda Sobey.

Brent Tradesmen

The staff of Salter & Son, bespoke tailors, 1942. Left to right: John Salter, Ena Hawkins, Douglas Wills, Joy Lang, Barbara Sleep and Irvy Wood, with George Salter, the proprietor, sitting in the centre.

(EALES COLLECTION)

Mrs Catt's shop in Nelson Terrace. The shop in front of No. 3 was run by Mrs Catt first as a wool shop, then as a fish and chip shop. It then became a cycle shop where you could get an accumulator filled, and finally a general store selling everything from safety pins to bicycles. Mrs Catt also ran dancing classes in the Church Hall. Note the two-figure telephone number on the sign.

(CATT COLLECTION)

Douglas Johnstone with some of his customers outside the Treasure Chest in the 1980s. (CROSBIE COLLECTION)

South Brent Pharmacy in Church Street was founded by Mr Catford, who was succeeded by Mr S.F. Brockington. Mrs Woodhouse then took over and at the time of writing it is run by Mrs Kay Reynolds. This 1955 photograph shows Miss Thelma Hard, for many years the principal assistant behind the counter. The inside of the shop has changed little since this picture was taken. Inset: The exterior of the Pharmacy in 2005.

Mr Arthur Manning's shop in Station Road in the early-twentieth century. (ANDERSON COLLECTION)

The demolition of the cottages at the bottom of Church Street, c.1960. Mr Maye is seen coming up the street as Mr Pulleyblank goes around the corner. Note the Police Station behind the lamp. (JOAN BROWN COLLECTION)

other side of the stairs was the butchery, manned at various times by Frank Newman, Jim Andrews and Hartley Bowden. Upstairs Miss Arnold ran the haberdashery and general goods department. Margaret has childhood memories of meeting Father Christmas (Mr Jefford) in his grotto at the top of the stairs, which for the rest of the year served as the fitting room! Next door Miss Thirza Hart ran the bakery, dairy and confectioner's. Miss Hart is remembered as being a very meticulous lady, especially over stock-taking, when she would count every sweet in every jar. It was a very successful and happy store. When other societies were giving a dividend of 3d. or 6d. in the pound, those at Brent and Buckfastleigh were as high a 9d. As well as the Co-op, Tidballs, Durbridges and the Central Stores all sold groceries and greengroceries. Hardware and building supplies could be purchased from Cranch's. There were two banks, Lloyd's and Barclay's, two independent butchers, White's and Winzer's, Miss Manning's paper shop, Brockington's pharmacy and Mayno Hayman's haberdashery shop. Tuckers ran a bakery.

One of the main informal meeting places in the mid-twentieth century was Andrews's fish and chip shop in Church Street. Nora Andrews ran it with help from her sister, Lottie Knapman, under the

watchful eye of Mrs Andrews and Vida from the sitting-room at the back. As well as serving fish and chips and 1d. or 2d. drinks made up in appropriately sized bottles, the shop sold a whole range of groceries and general goods as well as lighting sticks and paraffin – a real 'general store'. Nora Andrews was one of the first in Brent to have a car, which she used to collect her stock. For a short time Huxtables ran a rival fish and chip shop further down the road at No. 1 The Exchange. The gas-works at Brent Mill was run by Mr Saunders.

... With a Very Busy Junction...

The railway junction at Brent was a very busy place in the middle of the twentieth century, when locals would travel all over South Devon by rail.

Before the Second World War it was possible to leave Brent by the 4.50p.m. train, go to Plymouth, do the weekend shopping and return to Brent again by 8p.m. Even after the war it was possible to catch the train, often pulled by a Southern Region Battle of Britain class engine, at 3p.m, travel to Newton Abbot and be back in Brent again by 5p.m. On early-closing day there was always a knot of people, having paid their 4s. fare, waiting for this train. The southern region engine was used in order to familiarise drivers with the western region track in case of an emergency.

The staff at Brent Station during the Second World War. Standing, centre left is Mrs Helen Moores.

(MITCHELL COLLECTION)

Brent Station as it was in its heyday before closure and subsequent demolition in 1964. Top: The main entrance showing the footbridge; above: looking towards Higher Station Bridge on the up platform.

(KEN WILLIAMS COLLECTION)

Top: *Staff on the branch-line platform at Brent Station in the early 1950s. Left to right: Frank Spiller, Bill Manning, Mr Reynolds, Mr Roper and Bill Selley.*

(PINHEY COLLECTION)

Above: *Bert Field in the Brent signal-box, early 1950s.*

(FIELD COLLECTION)

On Newton Abbot market-day, farmers from the moors would catch the 10a.m. train, leaving their ponies and traps in the car park at the front of the station building and collecting them on their return at 3p.m. Summer Saturdays were a particularly busy time. Trains from London would call at Brent full of holiday-makers bound for a summer break in Cornwall. When the train arrived in Brent it would have one or two carriages bound for Kingsbridge. These would be uncoupled and the main train would continue its journey westwards. The Kingsbridge-bound coaches, having been shunted around, would then be coupled to the branch train for the final stage of their journey. Similarly, Paddington-bound trains from Penzance would stop at Brent, where the through coaches from Kingsbridge, ready in the siding over the river, would be shunted forward and coupled to the main express for their onward journey.

Apart from the activity on fair days, when cattle and ponies from the drift would be despatched from the station, many other goods would leave from the goods shed. The carter in the early years of the twentieth century was Mr Bunny Andrews, well remembered as carrying flock bound for Huddersfield from the mills on his horse and cart, as well as any other goods that needed to be sent by rail. The horse also did duty with Mr Shillabeer, for the early cutting of the grass down at Somerswood, to keep down the flies that irritated the horses, and also by 'Nutty' Newman who, as the scavenger, would take the refuse down to the tip at Quarry Park. Graham Jordan notes:

In this day and age of road transport, it is hard to imagine that practically every item of goods (food, iron-mongery, building materials clothing and the like) was despatched by a daily goods train, rarely named a 'freight train' from the manufacturers to the goods shed at Brent.

In the 1950s there was occasionally great excitement among the train-spotters sitting by Higher Station Bridge when the train stopping at Brent was pulled not by a familiar steam engine but by one of the gas-turbine engines introduced at this time. One of the most enthusiastic of those train-spotters was Mickey Salter, who would spend hours by the wall over-looking the station collecting engine numbers.

Bert Field tells of the time when he came into the station early and was fiddling with the gaslights. He was shocked to find a 'gentleman of the road' – nothing visible but his nose – sheltering on the station bridge which, being enclosed on the western

An aerial view of the Avon Dam.   (AEROFILMS LTD)

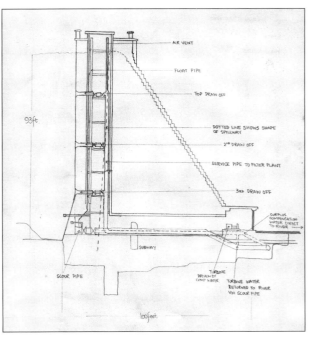

A cross-section plan of the Avon Dam.

side, acted as a perfect windbreak. The tramp was asked to leave and did so quietly, taking his pram with him.

On another occasion two rams were brought up on the train from Kingsbridge and were 'packed' around their rear quarters so that they would not make a mess. They were brought off the train and were to be tied in the parcels office to the leg of a table which was fixed to the floor. They were taken across the wooden crossing on the downside of the platforms, Ernie Choak holding one of the rams and Bert Field the other. As they came up onto the up platform Ernie Choak's ram took fright and bolted down the platform, dragging Ernie along on his stomach, with Mark Roper, the leading porter, in hot pursuit. They eventually managed to stop the ram and all was well.

Bert tells of his experiences in the signal-box:

A bell would ring from Tigley box at Rattery on the down line, or from Wrangaton on the up, which told us that there were about eight or nine minutes for a passenger train to pass. There were 63 levers in the box and they controlled the cattle pens, the signals for the loops and the up and down loops in addition to the signals. There was a token machine for the Kingsbridge branch with a key that prevented two trains being on the branch at once by locking the signals. They were switched over at Gara Bridge with one token controlling the Brent to Gara Bridge section and the other the Gara Bridge to Kingsbridge section. The loops enabled any train to be put to one side whilst a faster one went through. On summer Saturdays there were through coaches to and from Kingsbridge that were shunted into the sidings before being connected to the up trains.

Bert adds that Brent Station was 'a busy old place'.

David Carroll recalls an accident at the lower railway bridge (Hawkes Bridge), when a goods train came off the line and shed its load of barrels, inevitably closing the line for a short period. He also remembers the sound of the pump which brought water up from river level into the water-tower by the bridge.

... and a Dam Built Upstream

The idea of building a dam across the River Avon to create a reservoir was first suggested as early as 1948, before the South West Devon Water Board came into being. The enquiry into the building of the dam took place late in 1949. With much controversy and with problems over the planning, the Minister finally gave his consent in 1950. The chairman of the Water Board, Mr Robert Prowse, cut the first sod of earth on 16 September 1954. Mr Roland Lewis can claim to be the first workman on the site, as he was responsible for bringing timber across the moor for Foster Deacon, of North Huish, who was sinking the first boreholes. The first of the construction team was Norman Herd, who started in the spring of 1954. One of the first tasks for contractors Tarmac Ltd was to build a road from Brentmoor House out to the dam site for the transportation of everything from materials to personnel. A large workforce was brought in from all over the area, with Millman's Coaches bringing those from Torbay and Embankment Coaches bringing those from Plymouth. Some men came in from Dartmouth on coaches run by Couch & Stoneman and, of course, there were workmen from Brent.

Normal working hours were from 8a.m. to 5p.m. with 30 minutes for lunch and two ten-minute

The SBADS 1977 production of Emlyn Williams's psychological masterpiece Night Must Fall, *featuring* (left to right) *John Parr, Jane Tuson, Jenny Prince, Zoë Clough and Jenny Pickering.* (SBADS COLLECTION)

breaks, at 10a.m. and 3p.m. A small night shift prepared the work for the next day, starting at 8p.m. and working a 12-hour shift. Some Brentonians can still remember hearing the blasting out at the quarry site, where Raymond Male was the shot-blaster.

The foreman was an Irishman, Tommy Walsh, who would walk around the site in a white coat. Bob Wright, who worked on the site, remembers Tommy 'feeling for a light bulb in the darkness and plugging himself in.' Fortunately, 'he was found intact except for the tips of two fingers.' Although it was hard work building the dam, there was great camaraderie.

Bill Martin, who ran the Anchor, won the contract for the canteen and employed Doll Trundle and Gertie May to run it – the only women on site. The food was sourced from Brent and is reported to have been very wholesome.

The dam is curved to a 1,200ft radius with a length of 870ft and a 120-ft spillway in the centre. In places the foundations are 12m. deep. A total of 30,500 cubic yards of soft material was excavated from the site, along with 50,000 cubic yards of rock, and 1,500 tons of concrete were used in the dam's construction. Bob Wright comments:

During some periods we moved 500 cubic metres of concrete per shift. The batching plant delivered concrete

in six ton skips which were hauled into position on a 'Bailey bridge' erected across the dam. The granite pieces were larger than in normal concrete and pushing it around all day wasn't easy. As all the blocks were made on site, the batcher had to provide for that as well.

Entertainment

Many people in Brent can remember one of the highlights of the week being the Friday night travelling cinema in the Church Hall. It was very popular, with the queues to get in winding their way around the Church Hall. Ernie Catt, who was the projectionist, recollects setting the hall up for the customary double bill, of which the second feature was often a western. He remembers the proprietor's Great Dane, which always came with him. The 'balcony' was set up on the stage, as was the projector. Gwen England recalls that seats cost 1s.6d. and 1s.9d., though all cinema-goers sat on the same hard seats facing the screen, which was on the wall above the main doors.

Brenda Vallance remembers that she and her husband Dennis would spend many pleasant hours playing tennis in the courts at Oak House. She also recalls that people would go for walks around the lanes and by-ways of Brent – as many still do. The Vallances were also members of the South Brent

At South Brent Badminton Club are Inez Smeeth, Queenie Wakeham, Ernie and Margaret Catt and Valerie Catt.

(CATT COLLECTION)

Badminton Club, which Ernie and Margaret Catt remember as a very large and thriving concern. The matches played against other clubs were mainly friendlies, although in later years the club joined a league. Queenie Wakeham is remembered as being an active member into her seventies.

There was also SBADS, of course, the South Brent Amateur Dramatic Society. The late 1950s saw the beginnings of something of a golden age for SBADS, with the group winning a major award in the Paignton Drama Festival with *Boy on the Corner*, and the Fred Smart Silver Cup coming to Brent for the first time. The 1960s began with another triumph at the festival with *Ride a Tiger*, but the golden age began to fade, with audience numbers dwindling and a shrinking membership, and towards the end of the decade there were moves to wind up the society. It finally went into 'hibernation', until Mrs Carol Davies took the chair in 1972.

In 1963 Carol, an accomplished actress, had produced André Obey's play *Noah* with one of the village youth clubs. Her first production for the society came in 1966, with *Pink String and Sealing Wax*. She had fought to keep the society going during its period in the doldrums and was now to turn its fortunes around.

Maggie Taylor writes:

Exactly how she did it nobody knows, not even Carol herself. But somehow or other, do it she did, and the whirlwind speed at which she did it must have been wondrous to behold. Committee meetings returned to

Summer afternoon at Shipley for Bill Watts, Nano O'Connell, Margaret O'Shea, Christine Joint and Rose Watts. (CROSBIE COLLECTION)

being regular as soon as she took her place in the Chair, and within the space of a couple of months society meetings were being held every week, fund-raising events were up and running again, two social evenings had taken place, as had a summer party, and Mrs Davies had even managed to start a SBADS youth section.

More than that, she pressed ahead with the idea of putting on a play before the year was out. It wasn't going to be easy, Tony Bott volunteered to produce it and Les Kidger agreed to be stage manager, but the Society still had very few members and Carol had to go head-hunting for actors and back-stage workers alike, a job that stretched even her remarkable powers of persuasion to the limits. There was also the question of the lights and flats that had been given to what was now the Village Hall: someone would have to go cap-in-hand and beg to borrow them back. But elbowing aside all these obstacles, the new Chairman hustled it through, and on December the 2nd 1972 SBADS presented Busybody, *its first production in nearly five years.*

For the faithful few who endured those years it must have been a moment of pure joy when the drama group appeared on stage again after being so long in the wilderness. And it must have been a moment of equally pure relief when the audience made its own appearance,

A 1956 pantomime with, left to right, standing: *Jean Stuart, Mary Preston, June Andrews, Margaret O'Shea, Sally Newman, Nano O'Connell, Anne Hayman;* front row: *Godfrey Stancombe, Leonard Sparkes, Ralph Arscott.* (PARSONS COLLECTION)

Cast from The Goose Girl. *Left to right back row:* Joan Mortimore, Nano O'Connell, Pam Smith, Betty Mortimore, ?, Ann Watts, Joyce Hughes, June Andrews, Roseanne Chandler, Jean Uren, Ruth Dodd, Margaret O'Shea, Rose Watts; *front row:* Pam Mores, Paula Hannaford, ?, ?, ?, Janet Dodd, ?. (PARSONS COLLECTION)

An early-1950s production of The Goose Girl, *featuring Pam Andrews.* (SALTER COLLECTION)

for the play was surprisingly well-attended and made a profit of almost £40.

In addition, the success of the play brought in new members, as Maggie notes:

Tom Anderson, Sally Cottis, Sue Burgess and Doreen Yates were all roped in for her production of The Brontës, *which went on stage in the following Spring, and seven months later Wendy Lance, Stella Gillingham and Paul and Mary Wonnacott made their stage debuts in* Brides of March, *again produced by Carol.*

So successful was the revival that by summer 1973 there were more people wanting to be involved than there were productions for them to be in.

In 1974 the society embarked on its most ambitious production to date, *Our Town*. It is remembered as being very adventurous for Brent, with virtually no scenery or props and many techniques that were new to the cast.

Sue Burgess remembers the play very well, not for its unusual features, but for a quirky occurrence concerning the trains on the railway line across the road from the hall, or rather one particular train:

It happened one evening when Sue and Robin Horan were happily beavering away with their parts of the young sweethearts Emily and George who were seated at their open bedroom windows and having a night time chat. Emily said to George, 'If you listen, you can hear the train all the way to Kantanook', at which point the London to Penzance express decided to get in on the act as well and belted by the hall to provide the play with a real live sound effect… It was dead on cue.

During the summer months many of the young people of Brent would gather either at Lydia Bridge or above the Crackhills weir, with plenty of old rubber inner tubes and tyres, to swim in the river. One of the exciting dares was to jump off the bridge

into the deep pool beneath. In order not to hit the rocks it was necessary to stand on an old iron bar that came out far enough to allow a straight jump!

Shipley Bridge was, and still is, a popular place to picnic in the summer, with rocks to sit on and swimming in the various deep pools along the River Avon. Brentonians old and young would flock out there, especially on Wednesdays, early-closing day, and on Sundays, when some would stay all day. During the winter months there was the Youth Club held in the Vicar's Hall at the bottom of Church Street.

At School in the Middle of the Century

In May 1960, Mr Sparkes organised a school trip to London. The party left school at 7.00a.m. and went by coach to Totnes, where they caught the train to London, arriving in the capital at 12.15p.m. Whilst in London they took a sightseeing tour around the city, including Marble Arch, Park Lane, Piccadilly, Hyde Park Corner, and Buckingham Palace, as well as other venues en route, ending up at Westminster Pier, where a trip was taken on the river to Greenwich. The return journey from Greenwich by road took in the Tower of London. Everybody had a meal in the Coventry Street Lyon's Corner House consisting of: fried egg, bacon, grilled tomatoes and fried potatoes; bread and butter and jam; fruit pie; tea.

The party then caught the 5.30p.m. train, which reached Totnes at 10.12p.m. and finally got back to Brent at about 10.30p.m.

At the 1963 annual school sports Mr Sparkes gave the children and parents various items to sell. This launched a massive fund-raising effort to provide a wooden-framed, plastic-lined swimming pool in the school playground. Both children and parents held various events and, together with donations received, £280 was raised towards the cost of well over £500, with Devon County Education Committee granting a further £250. Mr Sparkes and Mr Clemens, his deputy, erected the pool which, at 25ft long and 17ft wide, was really a training pool. The

Carnival Royalty

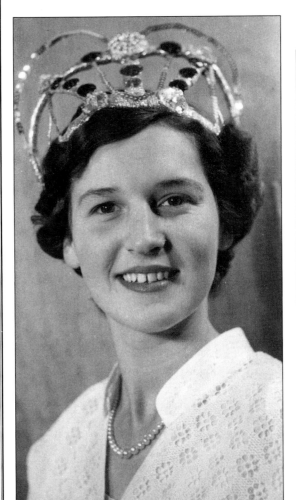

Pam Andrews.

David Newman, carnival prince in 1956, remembers going with Captain Raikes in his Morris Minor to get the carnival queen, Ruth Dodd, and her attendants, Ruth Giggs and Janet Nesaule, who had been chosen by Pat Jones, a former Plymouth Argyle player. He also recalls having a cream tea at Millswood, the Raikes's home, and starting the carnival ball by dancing with the queen, even though he only came up to her waist. The costumes were made by Mrs Sheila Wall and Hawke's coal lorry, cleaned by David's father, 'Nutty' Newman, and Bill Hockaday, after the Saturday morning deliveries, was decorated with rhododendrons.

(DAVID NEWMAN COLLECTION)

The crowning of the 1957 South Brent carnival queen by Mrs Bernice Gray, the Mayoress of Totnes. The carnival queen that year was Jean Uren, and her attendants were Serena Soper, Pauline Newman, Kenneth Jordan, Marilyn Langdon and Avril Trundle. (MILLER COLLECTION)

The carnival float in 2001, when Alison Parr was carnival queen.

Pupils of South Brent Primary School with their teacher, Mrs Hughes, 1957. (VALLANCE COLLECTION)

Mandy Langdon, Brenda Vallance, Brenda Miller, Phyl Rundle, Val Wollington, school mealtime assistants in the 1970s. (VALLANCE COLLECTION)

The school football team, 1958/59. Left to right, standing: Mr Sparkes, Dennis Hoare, John Palmer, Terry Jordan, Anthony Beable, ?, David Sandry, Michael Hall, Mr Bewdley, Brian Male; seated: Stuart Witheridge, Billy Skelton, Douglas Langdon, Barry Male, David Wild. (VERA JORDAN COLLECTION)

cost was practically covered by the time of its opening in July 1964. Miss E.A. Pearse, who had been a teacher at the school for over 40 years and who regularly acted as recorder for sports days, was

The lower junior class at South Brent Primary School, 1954.

The prizewinners in the school pancake-day races, 1974. Standing: Lawrence Mant, Margaret Karkeek, Bernard Langdon, Michael Smith, Alan Lake, John Wain (head teacher), ?, Marilyn Smith, Mandy Fox, Mary Wonnacott; seated: Debbie Langdon.

(WONNACOTT COLLECTION)

asked to perform the ceremony. Still well-remembered in the town, Miss Pearse said in her speech:

I have heard that you have all worked very hard and parents as well. I know you will love your swimming lessons. I wish I was young enough to start, but you will probably become very good swimmers beginning at this age. Maybe one or two of you will swim the channel or win a gold medal.

As she spoke the words, 'I declare the pool open', ten boys and girls jumped into the pool simultaneously.

Mr Sparkes retired in July 1968 and was succeeded by Mr Peter Feloy, who was head teacher until July 1978.

By 1972, South Brent Primary School had grown to such an extent that it occupied a split site which straddled Totnes Road, the middle and upper juniors having to cross the road frequently. Although the children were usually supervised, head teacher Mr Feloy pointed out that, 'There are odd times, at break or if a child is late, when they have to cross alone.' As a result both parents and teachers, with the support

Pupils of South Brent Primary School, 1960. Left to right, back row: *Margaret Cousins, Sarah King, Marilyn Burrows, Judith Luker, Caroline Mitchell, Jilly Skelton, Sandra Hocking, Carol Williams, Judith Trebble;* middle row: *David Thomas, Billy Oliver, Dorothy Collacott, Christine Field, Linda ?, Patsy Sabine, Adam Jellard, Roy Way;* front row: *Tony Skelton, Graham Williams, Brian Burns, Joseph Deville, Steven Johns, Michael Stevens, Ken Jordan.* (Vera Jordan Collection)

Pupils of South Brent Primary School, October 1960. Included are Hugh Boorman, Terry Bond, Martin Goss, Derek Luscombe, Trevor Newman, Elizabeth Wright, Paula Watts, Ann Waddams, Susan Sharville, Susan James, Richard Tapley and John Cranch. Their teacher is Mrs Hughes.

South Brent Primary School, 1974/75. Left to right, standing: *Vera Jordan, Rosemary Riddell;* back row: *Gary Langdon, Tina Haley, ?, Linda Mugridge, Alan Major, Jane Wakely, John Anderson, Christine Putt, Paul Honeywell, Mary Ann Levitt;* middle row: *Darren Wollington, ?, Kevin Lilly, Juliet Kocheye, Joe Lyne, Anita Winall, Peter Richardson, Julie Hazelwood, Theresa Neals, ?;* front row: *?, Nigel Beale, Gary Downs, Lyn Phillips, Elizabeth Sparkes, Joanne Kelly, Paul Langdon, Andrew Livermore, Mark Rooke, Derek Grills.*

(VERA JORDAN COLLECTION)

Support staff at South Brent Primary School, 1970. Left to right, back row: *Lil Chandler, Sally Luscombe, Hazel Millington (kitchen supervisor), Ena Stephens and Val Wollington;* seated: *Marjory Wicks, Phyl Rundle, Brenda Miller, Peter Feloy (head teacher), Jean Miller, Vera Jordan.* (VERA JORDAN COLLECTION)

of the County Council, lobbied the Department of the Environment for additional road signs. They considered the signing in Totnes Road to be adequate. Mr Feloy's comments at the time were:

The road carries all the traffic from South Brent to Totnes. Soon the situation will be even worse because the lower road out of the village is to close to traffic temporarily and all the traffic in and out of the village will have to use the Totnes Road.

In April 1976, Mrs Lillian Chandler retired after 25 years working in the school kitchen and as a cleaner. She saw great changes in her time. She explained to the children at her retirement that when she first came to the school she had had to scrub the wooden tables in the kitchen every day, and that when she left everything was stainless steel and could be wiped down with a cloth. Two years later, in 1978, Mrs Hazel Millington retired as the kitchen supervisor.

On Being the District Nurse

The district nurse in South Brent between 1964 and 1971 was Julia Carroll, who trained in midwifery with Stella Gillingham, another South Brent resident. Julia came to Brent from Nottingham, having seen the post advertised. At first she was unable to drive and initially had to either walk or use buses to get to those who lived further afield. She took it upon herself to write to County Hall to ask if she might have a car and was delighted when they provided her with a Morris Minor. As she still had no driving licence, however, she had to find three responsible people to accompany her until she passed her test.

Bad weather was no deterrent to the district nurse – if there was snow it was on with the snow chains and away. Julia recalls a visit to a patient on the edge of the moor when, having driven as far as she could, she had to cross three fields in the snow to get to the house. Julia also recalls a time when, together with the Dartington district nurse, she ran ante-natal classes at Harberton. She and three pregnant ladies were on their way to a class when one of them saw, in a snow-covered field, a sheep unable to get off its back. Julia and the three mums-to-be got out of the car and went across the field to its aid!

The hospitality of the people of Brent is renowned. Nurse Carroll recalls visiting a Brent household one Christmas Day and being given a large festive libation. Although managing to drive back to her home in Corn Park, her tearful visit to a patient later in the day caused some concern, until the reason for her condition was explained.

The 1960s and the Demise of the Railway

In 1961 there were 12 up and eight down trains a day and six each way to Kingsbridge. As a result of Dr Beeching's policies, however, first the Kingsbridge branch and then inevitably Brent Station were threatened with closure.

The demise of the branch line was confirmed when, in July 1963, a public notice appeared outside the station announcing that:

With the consent of the Ministry of Transport, the British Railways Board hereby give notice that on and from Monday 16th September 1963, the local passenger and freight train service between Brent and Kingsbridge will be discontinued together with the through passenger trains between Kingsbridge, Totnes and Newton Abbot and the line between Brent (exclusive) and Kingsbridge (inclusive) closed for all purposes.

The Western National Omnibus Company Limited already provide road services in the area covered by the branch line and additional services will be introduced on and from Monday 16th September 1963.

The final trains on the line ran on Saturday September 14 1963. Shortly afterwards the track was lifted, putting an end to any dreams of turning the branch into a tourist steam railway. Bert Field, who enjoyed his time working on the railway, had been a relief signalman working boxes all over South Devon, ending up as a special-class signalman. It was Bert who signalled the last train on the branch line and who had to operate the closing trains that went down to clear out the furniture – a sad time for all.

With stations between Plymouth North Road and Brent already gone, that at Brent was soon to suffer a similar fate. The siting of Brent Station on the farther edge of the village meant that most Brentonians had easier access to the main road buses than to the trains.

And so on 31 July 1964, a year after the announcement of the closure of the branch, a notice was posted outside the station announcing that the Minister of Transport had given his consent to its closure, adding that 'only one in six of the people who use public transport from Brent travel by train'.

Letters from Brent WI protesting at the closure were sent to the Parish Council, the transport users' committee and to the WI county secretary to ask if the county would lend its support, but this was one fish too big for the ladies to tackle. In September the black and white announcement of the date of closure was posted on the board outside the station:

With the consent of the Ministry of Transport, The British Railways Board hereby give notice that on and from Monday 5th October 1964, railway passenger services will be discontinued from the following station: BRENT.

The Western National Omnibus Company, and The Devon General Omnibus and Touring Company already provide services in the Brent area and details can be obtained on application from the Omnibus Companies concerned.

Arrangements for the collection and/or delivery of parcels traffic in the area will be maintained.

It was signed by the general manager, G.F. Fiennes.

The last train to stop at Brent Station arrived from Plymouth in fading light on Saturday 3 October 1964. The few passengers who got off the train on this sad occasion handed their tickets to Mr Jack 'Dingy' Garland, railway porter at Brent Station for many years. Then, with a couple of blasts on her whistle to mark the occasion, the train pulled out of Brent Station for the last time – a sad sight. In the silence, Jack Garland walked around putting out the gaslights, leaving the station in darkness. Soon even freight traffic ceased, and before long the platform buildings were demolished and the rails in the goods yard ripped up. So ended 116 years of railway history in Brent.

Beating of the Bounds

The beating of the bounds is an ancient ceremony that has survived in this country for hundreds, if not thousands, of years. The beating of South Brent's boundstones takes place every seven years and alternates between the inner bounds – the boundary with North Huish, Diptford, Harberton and Rattery – and the outer bounds, which go up onto the moors and mark the boundary with Ugborough, Dean Prior and Lydford. The outer bounds stretch some 8.5 miles, inner bounds 13 miles, and the ceremony attracts many people. Young people are ceremonially bounced on a stone so that they will remember the bounds of the parish for the rest of their lives. At the end of the walk there is usually a ram roast to finish off the day.

Local poet A.H. Elliott wrote the following poem describing the events of the 1959 beating of the outer bounds, which took place on 8 August:

*Of all the age-old customs
That Brent Folks are so proud,
The Beating of the Parish Bounds
Is one that thrills the crowd,
Twelve miles of good old Dartmoor,
Over Hill and Dyke,
From Corringdon to Dockwell
To claim our Legal Right.*

*It's thirteen years since last we trekked
Across yon dreary Moor,
Most stalwarts of those good old days*

Outside the Avon Inn at Avonwick during the beating of the inner bounds. Left to right: Harold Hard, Mr and Mrs O'Shea, Geoff Hard, George Preston, Trevor Jones and (standing at the front) Jill Hard. (CROSBIE COLLECTION)

Top: *The beating of the outer bounds in Edwardian times.*
(CRANCH COLLECTION)

Above: *Beating the bounds on 18 September 1948 are,*
left to right: *Mr Dodd, Roland Lewis, Roy Pearce, Stan*
Stephens, John Wild, Bill Goodman, Jenny Goodwin and
'Tiddler' Heard on Champagne.
(WILD AND FROOM COLLECTIONS)

Top: *The beating of the outer bounds in 1919.*

Above: *Norman and Melba Hard at Western Whita-*
burrows during the beating of the outer bounds, 1959.

Are – alas – with us no more,
And as I pen these words of mine
My heart just missed a beat
That Anno Domini should cause
Me missing such a treat.

The Council too deserve our thanks
For progress is their theme,
To claim the rights Brentonions love
Is not an idle dream,
Invitations were sent out,
There adverts made it clear
The Menu was of 'roasted Ram'
Washed down with Tea and Beer.

At 11.15 the starter's Flag
Was hoisted to the mast,
The Chairman read the 'Riot Act'
And Rules were duly passed,
As I surveyed this mighty throng
You'll please excuse my laugh
They came from all walks of Life,
Their 'Goal' was Ram and Draught.

The Water Board, I must admit,
Made everything so clear,
By leaving all the gates ajar

We had no trouble here,
The only snag, I must confess,
Gave our Yachtsmen quite a shock,
They'd hoped to get some practice in
For the 'Tommy Lipton's Cup'.

The Morning News *and* Daily Mirror,
The BBC and all,
Despite the strikes and short of ink
Responded to the call,
Rumours too, all proved quite false
About our dear old 'Ram',
Some said he's seen the Dentist
Or fallen in the 'Dam'.

The Women's Institute were there,
You'll always find them willing
To pull their weight in times of stress
As the tea cups they were filling.
The 'Specials' too so neat in blue
Cleared every traffic jam,
But to my surprise their longing eyes
Were focused on that 'Ram'.

Alas the marchers were in sight
To be greeted by a roar,
Congratulations handed round

The beating of the bounds, August 1985.
(INEZ JORDAN COLLECTION)

Speeches in galore.
Red Cross Workers set to work
But few casualties were seen
Some nice clean socks for aching feet
And the Rider's Vaseline.

The Council stakes caused quite a thrill
Eight runners at the post favourite
With 'Body Snatcher' close,
'Lever Puller' looked quite fit
And so did 'Esso Boy'
But a Lady member won the race
To every Punter's joy.

So we came to the end of a perfect day,
And the end of a journey too,
Our Chairman 'A' and good old 'Jack''
All kind thanks to you,
If an 'OBE' or 'KC.'
In honours come our way
There was no sham, with Beer and Ram
The Heroes of the Day.

Didworthy Closes

'The Cure that Killed a Hospital' was the headline which announced the closure of Didworthy Hospital in 1962. The account began evocatively:

When an ambulance cruises down the three miles of winding lane from Didworthy Hospital to South Brent next Monday carrying the last patient out of Didworthy Hospital, it should be the sound of trumpets, the hurrahs of the populace and the triumph of medical staff. It will not – although it will be an outwards and visible sign that medicine has conquered a killer. In fact, it could be amid the protests of nurses and doctors, taxpayers and ratepayers.

Although the staff thought it a great blunder to close a hospital that had been open for over 60 years, the nursing officer, despite advertising, had had difficulty in finding new staff. There had been no applicants which, together with the imminent retirement of

some of the senior staff, led to the decision to close.

Didworthy was purpose built when tuberculosis was rampant. The only treatment known was surgery, complete rest and lungfuls of pure fresh air. Specially designed wards and huts were erected that let in the pure Devon air summer and winter. Some were open at the sides. Some patients even slept under the open sky in summer.

Barbara Field, who worked at Didworthy, noted that this was the case for local people who suffered from tuberculosis and went to other such hospitals for a change of air.

The discovery of modern drugs such as streptomycin reduced the number of TB patients needing Didworthy by more than a half and other uses for the hospital were considered. One suggestion was to establish the building as a unit for minor orthopaedic operations, relieving pressure on Plymouth's Mount Gould Hospital. This actually worked well, but with the concentration of control in remote Plymouth, 'the strong feeling of dedication and loyalty that is bred in isolation and doing a rewarding job for its own sake began to break down.' The cost of running the hospital was also a consideration. The average cost per patient per week at Didworthy was £72.44, which was considerably higher than the average for Plymouth hospitals. This, coupled with the issues of

Barbara Stancombe and Margaret Thomas with Elizabeth, a patient at the hospital, in 1950 outside Didworthy Hospital, where Matron Hutchinson had a reputation for being very strict. (FIELD COLLECTION)

the distance from Plymouth and the reduction in the number of patients, spelled the end of Didworthy as a hospital.

In 1966 it was proposed to establish a unit for maladjusted teenagers at Didworthy. Dr Francis Pilkington, physician superintendent at Moorhaven Hospital, gave an assurance to concerned residents that there would be no danger as far as the public were concerned.

At a meeting of the Totnes Rural District Council, Captain K.E. Gordon, the Morleigh representative, who lived at Zeal Cottage, expressed concern at the scheme. Dr Pilkington revealed that:

... the unit would be for adolescents of both sexes between the ages of 13 and 17. There would be 24 beds and the sort of person selected for treatment would be maladjusted but not abnormal. Three months would be the average length of stay and there would be no danger to the public. The unit would be administered by one of the hospital management committees. One of the most important things was that the treatment was aimed at preventing mental illness or delinquency later in life.

A Brent councillor, Major-General Victor Campbell, noted that the matter had been discussed by the Parish Council and that they appreciated the concern felt by local residents.

Cllr Charles Jasper said that people in the locality were not so much afraid of the hospital's future use but the amount of freedom the patients were likely to get. The Parish Council had written to the Plymouth Hospital Management Committee asking for every precaution to be taken to safeguard people in the area. The Hospital authority has set aside £20,000 for the project and if Didworthy were to be chosen then Dr Pilkington added it would be two or three years before the scheme got underway. During treatment the teenagers will be able to play pop music as loud and as often as they like and they will get judo, badminton and squash instruction.

In the event, Didworthy closed 'temporarily' in 1971.

The WI Continues to Thrive

In 1961 Mrs H.M. Butler, the WI president, proposed that the WI should contribute something to the village to help improve its beauty. It was at the March meeting that year that members heard a Plympton gardener, 'Pop' Welsh, speak of the beauty of trees and how they could improve the landscape of the Devon roads. From that meeting the members decided that they would like to do something about a stretch of the Exeter to Plymouth road at the entrance to the village, which they felt was not exactly attractive. They sought and received permission from Devon planners and set about raising

A WI Christmas party in the 1960s.

(INEZ JORDAN COLLECTION)

money for the project. Originally it was hoped that an avenue of trees would line the way right into South Brent, but as each tree was to cost between £10 and £15 this was shelved and it was decided that the trees would be placed on the bend of the road opposite the Police Station, with a single tree planted in the playing-field at Sanderspool Cross. The planting ceremony was arranged for 7 December and was performed by Mrs Butler, with local civic dignitaries in attendance. The trees – two flowering crabs, three red oaks, two flowering thorns, a horse chestnut and two rowans – were to be planted and looked after by 20 children from South Brent, who were told by Mrs Butler at the ceremony to 'look after these trees and see that nobody does them any harm.'

Outings, parties, coffee mornings and fund-raising events were all part of the life of the WI at this time. Some of the highlights recorded include a visit to Buckingham Palace by a member whose name was chosen from those placed in a box. The lucky winner was Mrs Smeeth, who attended the garden party given by the Queen to celebrate the national WI jubilee year in 1965. On 3 May 1965 members enjoyed a day-trip to Holland. With a 5a.m. start from South Brent, 36 members and friends went by coach to Exeter and then by plane for a very full and interesting day in Holland. The tired but very happy party arrived back at Exeter Airport at 11p.m. Because of the interest in and support of this trip a day's outing to Paris was arranged the following year.

In 1970, a special meal was arranged to celebrate the South Brent WI golden jubilee year. A menu was printed and, with food prepared by members, the entertainment was provided by Mr George Farley of Plymouth, who gave an amusing display of magic and old-time variety.

After years of use, the old hut which had been home to the both the WI and the Girl Guides, and which had given hours of pleasure to village residents, finally gave up. At the February meeting in 1972 members were asked to note the state of the hut and to vote if they agreed to further meetings being

Bing Crosbie, Pat Crosbie, Rosalie Smeeth, Margaret O'Shea and Pam Andrews enjoying an evening out.

(INEZ JORDAN COLLECTION)

held in the Village Hall. This was agreed and arrangements were made for the hut to be disposed of and for the Guides to be notified. Mr Tom Anderson of Higher Downstow agreed to undertake the dismantling of the hut, which measured 80ft by 16ft, and to clear the site. The committee members made a list of things they felt would be useful and members were asked if they agreed to them being given to the Village Hall. Among items taken from the hut was a globe presented to the Institute by Mrs Collier in December 1961, which was placed on a bracket over the main hall inner entrance. With the move from their own hut to the Village Hall an important chapter in the history of Brent WI came to a close. Although the plot on which the hut had stood was designated for building, it was never developed.

The hut, while Tom Anderson was dismantling it, however, gave up some interesting secrets. A message and a regimental number were discovered, written on the wood in French and Flemish by one Francis J. Keyzereersch, a member of the 26th Regiment from Brussels, who was wounded at Castel Jodel D'Anver on 4 October 1914. The inscription seemed to suggest that the WI hut was used as a convalescent home during the First World War. Another find was a lapel pin, with a picture of a politician and the inscription 'We will stand by Ulster'. Mr Anderson suggested that this dated from around 1910 and was connected with the Irish troubles at a time when many officers resigned their commissions to go and fight in Ulster.

The WI have always taken an interest in national affairs. Without entering into politics and religious issues they have helped with numerous pleas and projects. One notable example was when the WI, at national level, campaigned for the removal of turnstiles from ladies' toilets – most of them are now gone. Just one example, but nevertheless an interesting one. The national AGM, held in June at the Albert Hall in London, has a representative from every WI in the country and the resolutions discussed are for the benefit of everyone.

A Changing Administration

At the end of the 1960s and the beginning of the 1970s changes were put forward which would have radically affected South Brent, which at the time was a civil and ecclesiastical parish within the Totnes rural district of the county of Devon.

The Redcliffe-Maud Report is the name generally given to the report published by the royal commission on local government in England 1966–1969 under the chairmanship of The Rt Hon. Lord Redcliffe-Maud. The commission was given the task of looking at the structure of local government in England and making recommendations for change.

Initially the report did not make any proposals to move South Brent from its existing position as part of the Totnes area. It proposed that a new 'unitary authority' be set up to take in the Tavistock, Plympton St Mary and St Germans Rural District Councils, as well as those of Torpoint and Saltash. However, the Plymouth City Council's finance and policy committee took the view in June 1970 that the boundary of the new authority should be extended eastwards to include both South Brent and Ugborough, both of which were part of Totnes Rural District Council, and went so far as to include 26 other parishes in the South Hams. The argument was centred on the fact that the two parishes would straddle the proposed new dual carriageway, placing them within 20 minutes of the city and that the residents of both places:

... would be better served by being represented on a Plymouth Unitary Authority which would have a major effect on their economy and environment, rather than exist on the fringe, and having no voice in the decisions taken by the authority.

The reactions to these proposals were quick and obvious. Major-General Victor Campbell, chairman of the Parish Council and vice-chairman of Totnes Rural District Council and Mr Peter Moore, also of the District Council, led the opposition to the plan. The feeling in South Brent was that Plymouth should not be allowed to extend past the River Erme and that South Brent and Ugborough should stay as part of Devon. The Parish Council voted unanimously against the proposal and wrote to the Minister on the matter. Totnes Rural District and Devon County Councils supported the opposition. A change in national government meant that the plan did not go ahead, and in 1974 Plymouth became part of 'new' Devon and Brent's time with the South Hams District Council began.

At around the same time, a 67-page report issued by the county planning committee sought to plan ahead to define probable development, although it meant to set down no hard and fast rules. The survey took in the area between Torquay and Plymouth and

La Grand Place, Châteauneuf-du-faou, Brent's twin town.
(PACK HORSE COLLECTION)

A Co-op outing, c.1950.   (WOOD COLLECTION)

the northern part of the South Hams but concentrated on South Brent and Ivybridge.

The report, the work of Mr J.W. Turpin, divisional planning officer for south-west Devon, concluded that the population of South Brent had remained at about 1,800 during the previous 10 years and that a large proportion of the population were elderly retired couples. It was this category of person who was most likely to continue to move into the community. It continued by noting that Slumberland were the only manufacturers and that shops provided most of the service employment. The only land that could be released for development would be between the A38 and the proposed new bypass. The pressure for development in South Brent would not grow until land within the Plymouth boundary was fully developed and the population of Ivybridge reached 5,000.

Friendship across the Water

In 1977, the year of the silver jubilee of Queen Elizabeth II, South Brent was twinned with the French town of Châteauneuf-du-Faou. The friendship pact, translated by the French and signed by Peter Moore, then chairman of the Parish Council, and the Mayor of Châteauneuf-du-faou, records that:

In the town hall of Châteauneuf-du-faou on this twenty seven august of nineteen hundred and seventy seven
We the chairman of South Brent Parish Council
We maire de Châteauneuf-du-faou
Decree the twinning of the towns of South Brent (Devon) and Châteauneuf-du-faou (Finistere) with a view to promoting cultural, tourist, social and economical exchanges in the interests of both populations. Proclaim in the names of our townspeople, our intention to respect the intentions of the twinning charter in order to develop understanding, mutual respect and friendship between the inhabitants of South Brent and Châteauneuf-du-faou, thus preparing the way for peace and harmony among the peoples of the world in witness whereof.
We the chairman of South Brent Parish Council

We maire de Châteauneuf-du-faou
Have set our signatures and seals of our towns on this part.

St Petroc's Continues to Thrive

The biggest change to come about during the incumbency of Revd A.L. Vesey was the moving of the vicarage from its riverside location on the banks of the Avon to what became known as the Church House. Mr Vesey had long thought that the medieval building adjacent to the church itself, then known as the Manor House, would be an ideal site for the incumbent's residence and it was largely he who persuaded the church authorities to buy the building when Mr and Mrs Butler came to sell it. Thus the Church House became the vicarage and the old vicarage was sold, with a covenant that the land could not be developed, and Mr and Mrs Roper named it 'The Manor'.

There is an interesting anecdote about the vicarage and L'Aune path that runs beside it. There is a tradition that the ghost of a red cardinal is to be seen walking along the path. Mr Vesey was in the habit of taking his dogs with him when he went to say morning and evening prayers in the church each day. If he chose to walk to church along the river path the dogs would refuse to go with him, but would run up the drive and along Quarry Road and be waiting for him when he reached the end of the path. They would then quietly go with him to church. If he chose to go back by the river the dogs would go home via the road!

The comments about the state of the church during this period remain good and Mr Vesey, when he himself was elected rural dean, paid tribute to 'over 40 voluntary workers who dust and clean and scrub.'

On 31 August 1971 Mr Vesey retired from the benefice and Revd L.M. Malsom was instituted on November 17, having moved from the neighbouring parish of Harberton.

By 1973 the upper storey of the stables to the

Church House had been converted into the Church Room and, once again, St Petroc's had its own meeting place, the church hall having been sold to the village. In 1974 a new heating system was installed in the church and the local St John Ambulance cadet division had their flag blessed and lodged in the church.

In 1977 Revd David J.M. Niblett became vicar of South Brent in succession to Revd L.M. Malsom.

Brown Owl Retires

There are many ladies in Brent who will have fond memories of Miss Naomi Cranch who, when she retired from the organisation in 1977, had completed 50 years' service within the organisation. In March 1977 a ruling had been brought in that everyone was to retire at 65. Miss Cranch joined the Brownies in 1927 and, after training for six months and becoming a first-class Guide, was made Brown Owl. She served in that capacity until her retirement. During

Miss Cranch with her Brownies in the 1930s.

(EALES COLLECTION)

the Second World War Miss Cranch also took over the running of the Totnes branch when their captain was called to other things.

South Brent St John Ambulance Brigade in the late 1970s, including Colette Crosbie, Nicky Pike, Sally Fox, Lyn Warman, Julie Sparkes, Suzanne Mugridge, Teresa Wakeham, Neil Suddes, Andrew Rickard, Phyl Rundle, Lorraine Bass, Chris Miller, Barry Warman, Louise Hannaford, Robert Bayliss, Steven Bristow, Mr Bristow, ?, Delwyn, ?, Pauline Wicks, Sharon Sowden, Tracey Miller, Jayne Widdicombe, Denise Webber, June Wicks, Susie Towl, Fiona Sherlock, Jackie Pike, Ann Rush, Shaun Bass, Wendy Mumford, Sandra Cockings, Marion Stevens, Gillian Mead, Nicky Crosbie, Angela Hoare, Barbara Sparkes, Ann Wakeham, Doreen Hannaford, Anya Cockings, Susan Jordan, Jackie Towl, Loretta Bass, Ann Bennett, Ngaire Doye and Sally Rundle. (CROSBIE COLLECTION)

Brownie Revels, 30 June 1956, when the South Brent Pack went as pirates to Totnes. Left to right, back row: Miss Naomi Cranch (Brown Owl), Rosie Watts, Primrose Hunter; middle row: Ruth Bennett, Judith Luker, Nancy James, Carol Goss, Diane Wright, Janet Nesaule, Jean Sabine; front row: Marion Wills, Marilyn Langdon, Yvonne Wills, Daphne Hughes, Wendy Luker, Pat Bewsher, Marie Field.

(WOOD COLLECTION)

Youth Camps

Left: *The 1979 Methodist Sunday-school outing to the Shire Horse Centre.*

Right: *Scout camp. Left to right, back row: Brian Newman, Dennis Woods, Keith Miller, Brian Stone; front row: Paul Bennett, ?, Adrian Sharville, ?, Ian Davis, Colin Vallance, Gary Tidball, Adrian Harper.*

(VALLANCE COLLECTION)

South Brent Scouts in the 1920s, including Charlie Manning, Charlie Lang, George Smallridge, Fred Veale, Fred Soper, Hector Rogers and Bert Gill. (INEZ JORDAN COLLECTION)

A Methodist Youth Club outing in the late 1970s. Left to right: Patsy Sabine, Susan Hole, Jean Sabine, Roderick Tidball and Nick Sparkes.

(TIDBALL COLLECTION)

CHAPTER 8

The Parish Council Era, 1978–2005

An aerial view by Mike Sandry of South Brent at the time the Brakefield estate was being constructed.

(SANDRY COLLECTION)

The Fight for the New School

Mr John Wain took over the headship of South Brent Primary School at the beginning of the autumn term 1978 with such inevitable headlines as 'Put that pistol down, head!'. Mr Wain was born in Derbyshire and came to Brent from a 70-pupil primary school where he was the head teacher. He is quoted as commenting on arrival:

I was pleasantly surprised; everyone has been so helpful and understanding. My first week has been hectic. It has been difficult to find time to get to know the children while I have been finding my feet. However, once I have settled in that will be my prime task.

By the end of the 1980s the original Board School was starting to show signs of age. The school governors, under the chairmanship of Mr Guy Pannell, called for urgent repairs to be made to the leaking roof through which it was reported that water was running down the insides of the wall and making electrical switches dangerous, threatening the lives of pupils and teachers. Local newspaper reports stated that during periods of heavy rain 'the staff have to put buckets in these rooms to catch the water'. Even though £20,000 was spent in maintenance in one

summer, this had not remedied the problems in the Victorian main school and temporary buildings.

It was hoped that a new school building could be provided for South Brent in 1992/93. The governors and staff of the school were concerned that budgetary considerations in 1991/92 might well put back any new provision for the community. A total of 194 children were being taught in a building dating from 1876, and an additional five temporary classrooms. The school buildings occupied two sites on either side of Totnes Road, and Mr Wain considered them 'painfully inadequate'. At the end of the twentieth century some children still had to go outside to the toilets and most classes had to venture outside to get to the school hall – especially a problem during the autumn and winter, Brent being considered one of the wettest places in Devon.

By early 1994 it was reported that the end was in sight, and that the new school had been placed on the reserve list for county funding. This was greeted in Brent with cautious optimism, as this was only one of three reserve schemes that the County Council were asked to recommend at the time.

In February 1996 the headlines were: 'School's joy at 'one-site' decision'; '20-year battle pays off with £1m scheme' and 'Twenty-five year campaign for new school at South Brent finally pays off'.

135

Growing Up in South Brent

Gary and Amanda Tidball outside the former Sopers Garage in Totnes Road, 1986. (TIDBALL COLLECTION)

Bill Goodman and Eric Uren outside the front door of the toll-house at Brent Mill in the mid-1930s. (MILLER COLLECTION)

Christine and Mary Andrews outside 8 Wellington Square, 1932.
(ALAN JONES COLLECTION)

Michael Lucas, Amy Staddon, Jamie Wiggam, Sally Wiggam and Stella Gillingham at choir practice, 1990.
(CHOIR COLLECTION)

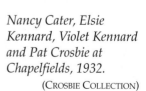

Nancy Cater, Elsie Kennard, Violet Kennard and Pat Crosbie at Chapelfields, 1932.
(CROSBIE COLLECTION)

Mrs Vera Jordan hearing Katie Williams read, March 1990. (VERA JORDAN COLLECTION)

In September 1996 came the news that work would begin on a new primary school for South Brent. Head teacher John Wain commented:

We are delighted and excited about getting a new school. I have been here for 18 years and during that time there has been work towards a new school. I have found evidence that there was talk of a new school back in 1970. It has been a long fight.

With the news that a new school was to be built a steering group was immediately formed to buy the Victorian building to develop as a community centre. For all the euphoria surrounding the decision, there was a sting in the tail. As the school budget would not be enough to staff all ten classrooms, there would be only eight, each class having as many as 35 pupils.

School governors and head teachers had previously met with Mrs Gillian Shepherd, Secretary of State for Education, over cuts that would lead to class sizes in South Brent Primary School rising to 30–35. Mr Anthony Steen MP arranged a meeting at which those who had to work with such policies could express the governors' points of view at the highest level. In 1995 the school lost a considerable amount of computer equipment in two burglaries.

There has long been a strong musical tradition in Brent. Reports in the local press show that South Brent Primary School has had creditable success in competitions and in providing entertainment for the adult community. In 1991 the school, under the guidance of Sue Steel, celebrated a second successive win in the Devon Youth Music Composition Competition with rugby song 'The Winning Machine'. The combined prizes amounted to £175.

In June 1995, in an OFSTED inspection, the school was reported to be above average in size for a primary school, having 255 pupils taught by 10 teachers, including the head teacher, with an average class size of 28. The school was described as:

... a good school with some excellent features. It is successful in promoting pupils' spiritual, moral, social

A school trip to Sparkwell, 1988. Those pictured include Mrs Noble, Richard Male, Mrs Hoare, Nicholas Hoare, Richard Wilding, Tessa ?, Gemma Savage, Marc McGee, Jamie Wiggam, Hannah Cooper, Mark Vinnecombe and Sean Biddis.
(VERA JORDAN COLLECTION)

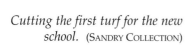

Cutting the first turf for the new school. (SANDRY COLLECTION)

The new school in 2005.

Three head teachers of South Brent Primary School, John Wain, Helen Nicholls and Peter Feloy. (SANDRY COLLECTION)

and cultural development. The school enjoys excellent relationships with the local community and with its parents. The atmosphere of the school is good.

The governors were set the task of improving standards of work and learning by looking at how the pupils' achievements could be enhanced by monitoring their work and reviewing the time allocated to the various subjects in the curriculum. The question of school buildings was also highlighted.

Although instrumental in the push to build it, and present when the first turf was cut, Mr Wain was not to be in charge when the new school was opened and retired in March 1997 after nearly 18 years in the post. One of his leaving treats was a ride in a Ferrari. One of the children was overheard to say, 'Is that what we saved up for?', as he was driven off.

Mrs Helen Nicholls became head teacher in September 1997 and the long-awaited new school was officially opened in May 1998 by the chairman of the County Council, Mr John Glanville. The original 1877 school bell was reinstated, helium balloons were released to mark the occasion and each child was presented with a commemorative mug. In addition

to a party, entertainment was provided by a Punch and Judy show and the Nappy Tappy Band from Plymouth's Estover Community College.

A Second Golden Era

Although South Brent Amateur Dramatic Society's fortunes have waxed and waned over the years, the time from the late 1970s onward has proved to be one of the high spots. In 1978 and 1979 SBADS became the first drama group to win the South Devon Drama Federation's top award for two consecutive years, with Jane Tuson's productions of *Relative Values* and *Love on the Dole*. The quality of the work produced by the group was further recognised when, in 1981, Paul Wonnacott won the best actor award for his portrayal of Major Pollock in *Separate Tables*. In 1984 *Not now Darling* won the best visuals award and in 1985 Veronica Brown's production of *Ladies in Retirement* was voted best production yet again, as well as winning the best visuals award, thanks to Mavis and Dave Hewitt's set and Gilly Hawes's costumes. In 1990 Veronica did it again, when *The Hollow* won best production and Sue Burgess scooped the best actress

The Village Hall Show

The WI have for many years taken part in the Village Hall concert, held every March to raise money to support the building. On stage are, left to right, *Pauline Juste, Margaret Eales, Margaret Catt, Win O'Connor, Wendy Woodley, Sylvia Warman, Rosemary Evans, Esther Warnes, Joy Hayman, Stella Stickland and Vera Bennett.*

(HAYMAN COLLECTION)

Guy van der Kiste, Francis Sparkes, John Wain, Peter Moore and Paul Wonnacott as gendarmes, 1985.

(WONNACOTT COLLECTION)

The Village Hall Gang Show, c.1980

Jack Garland, Jack Hard and Bill Endacott 'stood on Anchor corner'.

award. The highest accolades were not to bypass South Brent just yet, for in 1991 Carol Davies's interpretation of *The Miracle Worker* won best production and the young Hannah Hughes was especially praised for her portrayal of blind deaf-mute Helen Keller.

In 1992 Paul Wonnacott won another best actor award for Cathie Pannell's version of the Arthurian Comedy *A Spell of Virtue*. Although Cathie had great difficulty in finding a copy of the script, she finally managed to track one down to one of the co-authors, Charles Neilson Gatty, who attended the Saturday night performance. In 1993 Helen Ayres took the top award with *Top Girls*, with all eight of the cast nominated *en bloc* for the best actress award! It was in 1994 that SBADS broke all records at the Drama Festival when its production of *The Crucible* won three awards: Stella Hewitt for best production, Sue Burgess as Elizabeth Proctor for best actress (her second) and a new award, for best young performer, was spontaneously given to 14-year-old Gilly Ross for her portrayal of Mary Warren.

The SBADS repertoire was not confined to plays. In 1985 pantomime returned to the Village Hall when Mavis Hewitt produced *Jack and the Beanstalk*, followed in 1987 with John Palmer's debut as pantomime author with *Aladdin*, in which he also played Abanazar. The pantomime in 1989 was *Cinderella* and the society has produced a biennial pantomime ever since, John Palmer writing many of them. It was in 2001 that *The Sleeping Beauty* was produced for the second time, with many of the cast of the 1948 production there to see it.

The Recreation Ground

In 1982 the Parish Council, at a cost of £13,500, bought two fields on the Exeter road to develop into a high-standard sporting facility. In 1983 half of the old playing-field opposite the Police Station, owned by the Parish Council, was sold for development, raising £55,240. Of this, £2,000 was spent on improving the facilities to create a dedicated children's playground, £1,000 was given to the Village Hall to improve the facilities for the Youth Club, and the remaining £52,240 was allocated to the development of the new sports field. A total of £13,500 was spent in repaying the South Hams District Council loan for the initial purchase of the fields, and £18,240 on levelling and seeding the site and dealing with the associated legal fees and expenses. The sum of £8,000 was received from interest, grazing fees, tipping fees and the sale of surplus top soil. Despite problems caused by adverse weather at crucial periods, all the work was completed with the help of the Devon County Council's playing-fields experts.

In July 1984 the Parish Council handed over responsibility for the new site, together with the remaining £28,500, to the newly formed Recreation Association.

The aims of the association are:

To promote sporting and recreation facilities for the residents of South Brent and will co-ordinate the aspirations of the various groups seeking sporting and recreation facilities, including the provision of mutually beneficial facilities.

The committee, consisting of four parish councillors, one representative from each of the affiliated organisations and six other members, is elected by parishioners at the annual general meeting.

This committee then had the task of completing work on the pavilion, for which South Hams District Council were asked for a loan of £10,000. The Parish Council agreed to underwrite the loan and levy up to a halfpenny rate, if required, in order meet the repayments. In addition, the Sports Council gave awarded a grant of £1,500 in April 1987, together with a no-interest loan of £2,000 repayable over five years. However, money still had to be raised for a concept at the time described thus:

The Pavilion, when completed, will consist of four changing rooms, toilets, showers, a kitchen, a bar complete with store, a lounge and a general purpose store. The playing area has already been marked out with a senior football pitch, a junior football pitch and a cricket square. Space has been reserved for two tennis courts, a side/tennis/basketball/netball court, an area for petanque and ultimately a bowling green.

The cricket club, having lost the use of its previous pitch, intended to use the new field for the 1987 season. With the football club's future at the 'Marsh' uncertain, they also wanted to move to the new venue for the 1987/88 season. A massive fund-raising scheme was thus set in motion to ensure the building was secure by May 1987, with showers and changing facilities installed by September 1987.

The Anchor Fire – Disaster Overnight

The Anchor, one of Brent's Grade II listed buildings, stood at the junction of Fore Street and Station Road for hundreds of years. In 1990, however, the old building, built of wood and straw, was severely damaged by fire. The incident began with a hoax call

In 1990 the heart of the village was destroyed when the Anchor Hotel was gutted by fire, though luckily no lives were lost. These photographs were taken in the aftermath of the fire. Sadly, further demolition was necessary to render the building safe. (VERA JORDAN AND EALES COLLECTIONS)

Malcolm Tidball, 1990, organist at St Petroc's and else-where in the area for many years. (TIDBALL COLLECTION)

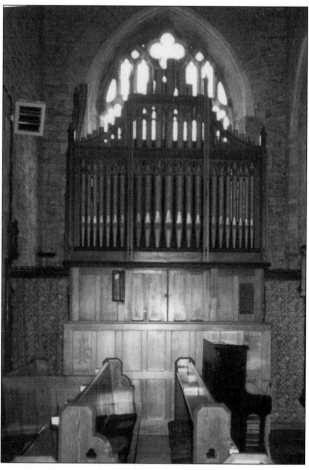

The church organ that was replaced.

at about 11.30p.m., two hours before the fire was discovered. Peter Lavers-Mason, manager of the hotel, made his final inspection at 1.30a.m. When his dog refused to go downstairs Mr Lavers-Mason opened the door to find that the building well alight. He, his wife Tracy and cousin Peter Eastley managed to escape with their pets before a gas cylinder exploded. The fire was so severe that it damaged the flat next door, which belonged to the Feoffees. The Anchor was eventually rebuilt to look exactly as it had before.

A potential disaster was averted in another of Brent's pubs in January 1994, when a fire in the chimney of the Pack Horse spread to an upstairs airing-cupboard through a hidden flue. Heat-seeking devices traced the fire's course.

Changes to Church and Benefice

During his incumbency Revd David Niblett hit national headlines when a comment he had made in the parish magazine appeared in *The Sun* newspaper. His comment that it was only necessary for commu-nicants to take a small sip of consecrated wine was taken up and interpreted as only a national tabloid can. Later the Niblett's son, Jeremy, appeared on the television show 'Blind Date'.

In 1978 a faculty was applied for to make major alterations to the tower. The bell-ringers had rung the South Brent peal from an area at the base of the tower that was screened from the rest of the church by a red curtain hung from a beam originally part of the medieval rood-screen. At the same time an increase in choir members meant that room in the vestry was very tight and it was decided to create a new ringing chamber and choir vestry in the tower by constructing a floor at first-floor level making a ringing chamber with a choir vestry underneath. The original plan, which gave access to the ringing chamber by way of an outside metal staircase, was refused in 1980 and it looked as if the whole project would be abandoned. However, by 1988 a new scheme, with an internal staircase leading from the new choir vestry, was approved and completed. The ringers were separated from the main body of the church by a glass screen. Following this, the pews at the west end of the church were removed to create a narthex – not to be used in the traditional sense for women, penitents and catechumens, but rather as an open area for refreshment and informal services.

At the end of Mr Niblett's incumbency, the ques-tion of the vicarage was once again raised. The Diocese of Exeter was keen to replace the Church House with a new building, bringing South Brent in line with the policy of having clergy houses that were less than 50 years old. As the Church House did not fall into that category, discussions began with the Parochial Church Council to determine what should be done. Apart from retaining the status quo – which would be least cost-effective – an option was to sell the Church House and build in its garden a new vicarage which might be linked to the Church Room. An alternative was to sell that plot for development and use the money to renovate the existing house. The third option was to buy a new house in another part of Brent and to sell the Church House to fund it. A major difficulty was the position of the Church Room, a very valuable asset to the church which might be lost if the vicarage moved. As time went on it became obvious that the preferred option was to sell the Church House and locate the vicarage elsewhere, whereupon the Parochial Church Council launched an appeal to buy the Church Room and the rooms underneath. At one stage the idea of the parish buying the whole building had been mooted!

A further issue on the retirement of Revd Niblett concerned his successor and the nature of his benefice. South Brent was unusual in 1991 in that it was one of the few parishes in the Diocese of Exeter not to share its incumbent. This was not to last for

much longer. In 1992 Revd John Harper came to South Brent and was first created priest-in-charge pending a pastoral review of the Totnes Rural Deanery which saw South Brent share its incumbent with another parish for the first time. The parish was Rattery, traditionally linked with Dartington and Brooking. John Harper, a Cornishman, came to Brent from Halsetown near St Ives, in the far west of that county, where he had been the incumbent since 1969. The start of his time in South Brent also saw the vicarage move from the medieval Church House to a new site in Hillside. Not long after he had moved into the new vicarage a giant pine tree fell through the roof, causing thousands of pounds worth of damage. Fortunately, Revd Harper and his wife, Romola, were not at home when the accident happened.

During Revd Harper's incumbency a new organ, originally from Christ Church, in Plymouth, where it had been built in 1884, was installed in the church. After its removal from Christ Church in 1966 by organ builders John Treliving and Maurice Eglinton, the organ was rebuilt in Plymouth's St Augustine's when some technical improvements were made.

The original organ in St Petroc's before it was moved to the north transept in 1946.　　　(Cranch Collection)

Golden Jubilee Celebrations, 2002

Crowds gather for the unveiling of the plaque.
(VERA JORDAN COLLECTION)

Cllr Peter Kelly, watched by the vicar of South Brent, Revd David Winnington-Ingram, unveils the base of the original jubilee lamppost, which was inscribed to commemorate the golden jubilee of Queen Elizabeth II. This joins the original inscriptions, firstly for Queen Victoria's diamond jubilee and then Queen Elizabeth II's silver jubilee.
(VERA JORDAN COLLECTION)

Shop windows decorated for the golden jubilee.
(VERA JORDAN COLLECTION)

With the closure of the St Augustine's Church a committee was set up under the chairmanship of Malcolm Tidball to raise the £25,000 necessary to bring the organ to St Petroc's. Amongst the fund-raising events was a concert by internationally famous American organist Carlo Curley. The new organ had the advantage of being at concert pitch, making it compatible with and able to accompany other instruments. With the St Petroc's organ sold, Hele & Co. were responsible for installing the new one, with Maurice Eglinton carrying out the work.

Another long-standing problem was solved during John Harper's incumbency. For many years the Parochial Church Council had been asked if toilet facilities could be provided in the church, the nearest available ones being in the Church Room and accessible only by a narrow flight of stairs. The major problem in providing such facilities in the church was of drainage, a problem that was overcome in 1997. It was decided to build an annexe on the north side of the door, on the site of a previous small building, with a connecting passage to preserve the medieval walls. The project meant the re-siting of the First World War memorial, which was placed with the Second World War memorial plaque in the south transept. The new facility became known as 'the garderobe' – a medieval lavatory often built into the thickness of a castle wall with an open drop to the moat below. As moths did not find the area attractive it was a good place to keep winter clothes, a place to 'guard the robes' from moths!

The initial drainage problem prompted Mr Tom Anderson to pen the following lines:

The Petroc Pong

The odiferous tide that with coffee appears
Would cause the most saintly to blush,
But its source is not us we would hasten to say
It's our brand new Episcopal Flush

Our drains have got twisted and won't run uphill
But who on earth thought that they should
A plumber might sort it but somehow I feel
That only a miracle would.

When John Harper retired from the incumbency on 30 June 1999, Tom Anderson penned another poem to mark the occasion:

John Harper

John Harper is our Vicar
He came from down St Ives
With Cornish charm and passion
To brighten up our lives.
His message from the pulpit
Left none of us in doubt
'I'll fill the church with people
And drive the devil out'.

His grandpa was a tinner
A mining captain he
John would visit lots of mines
Great wonders he would see.
He loved the deep bored mine shafts
with mud and tin and stone,
Then in his garden in St Ives
He found one of his own.

He really loved his rugby
To every match he'd go.
He had a unique style
Of slow, slow, stop, stop slow.
But now that he's retired and –
Hung up his rugby socks,
He gets his rucks and scrummages
From Sportsnight on the box.

A literary man is he,
From books he'd often quote.
Not only has he read them
Some of them he wrote
While he was courting Romola
Her only chance to speak
was when he stopped translating
The Bible from the Greek.

When Romola at last agreed
To be his blushing bride
He was strapped for cash
And had nothing put aside
So he went into the fields,
Digging bulbs at Secret's farm
To pay for the engagement ring
For his sweet, young, bright Schoolmarm

When John first came to join us
He had a lot to do
He was not the only Vicar
There was one in every pew.
What he had to deal with,
Nearly broke his heart in two.
So we sent him up to Tommy's
Where they patched him up like new.

He has many hobbies
Stone walls and carving wood
Drama and bell-ringing,
And hats, and well cooked food.
While walking his two boxers
You can smell his pipe afar
And after church on Sundays
He'll always clean his car.

Now you both are leaving
we wish you all the best
You're dashing off to Essex
To enjoy a well-earned rest.
You know that we will miss you

The staff of the Slumberland factory at Manor Mills. Left to right, back row: *F. Courtney, F. Newman, P. Field, R. Andrews, R. Smeeth, R. Luscombe, A. Hill, P. Stuart, J. Hill, A. Burgess, R. Couchman;* front row: *B. Chapple, D. Luscombe, T. Chapman, B. Chapple, ?, T. Hard, G. Wilkinson. The lady to the right of the picture has not been identified.*
(EALES COLLECTION)

*And pray that God above
Will keep you safely in his care
As we give you all our love.*

On Friday 21 January 2000 the Revd David Winnington-Ingram was instituted as 44th vicar of South Brent and 52nd vicar of Rattery.

Bell-ringers

The members of the South Brent Ringers Association have always been consistent in their efforts and have, over the years, achieved success in various ringing competitions, particularly in the 1990s. In June 1995 Linda Newman, Charles Hard, Ray Wakely, Trevor Newman, Ray Mugridge and Neil Holloway won the Ross Shield, a top trophy in Devon campanological circles, for the first time.

On Being the Village GP

Dr John Halliday, who came to the village to work with Dr John Parry just after the opening of the health centre, spent 30 years as one of South Brent's GPs. Dr Halliday recalls that in those days the two doctors knew everybody. With no appointments, there could be as many as 50 people in his surgery, who would see the doctor only when they reached the head of the queue! There was much consterna-

One of a pair of vases presented to South Brent by the people of Châteauneuf-du-faou to commemorate the twinning and now kept in St Petroc's Church.

(ADDY COLLECTION)

146

Dr John Halliday opening the carnival, 1981. Miss South Brent is Jackie Mitchell and her attendant is Anya Cockings. On the right is Fernley Rogers.

(WOOD COLLECTION)

tion when an appointment system was introduced – even the Parish Council felt obliged to write expressing its concern. By the time Dr Halliday retired in 2004, the health centre had expanded beyond recognition. At the time of writing there are six doctors supported by nurses, physiotherapists, a phlebotomist and office staff. Many patients who would once have been referred to specialists in Plymouth are now dealt with at the health centre – almost a mini-hospital in itself.

The life of a GP can be very rewarding and enjoyable and Dr Halliday can recall many interesting anecdotes from his 30 years. He was once called to a farm devoid of all modern comforts on the edge of the moor. Examining the old farmer, and feeling the cold coming up through the bedroom floor despite his stout walking shoes, the doctor got into bed with the patient to carry out his examination. On another home visit to an elderly patient he found what he thought was some kind of scab on the patient's forehead. Closer examination revealed it to be honey dripping though the ceiling from a wild bees' nest immediately above the patient's head! Although traditionally it is postmen who get bitten by dogs, sometimes doctors do, too, and Dr Halliday remembers examining a patient in a bed quite high off the ground when he was bitten by the dog concealed underneath it. The South Hams area has the highest proportion of home-births in the country, and the doctor recalls attending a mother who was always delivered in the same very small room. The close confines found him with his hindquarters stuck fast in the small fireplace behind him.

Living next door to a playground, Dr Halliday was amused periodically to hear, 'Hello Doctor!' from girls swinging high enough to see over the wall.

Commercial Enterprises

Before South Brent News was founded, the village newsagency was run by Miss Manning from her shop next to the Anchor in what, in 2005, is the Crumb and Cuppa tea-room. Bert Field has told us

The staff of South Brent News with, left to right, Esther Warnes, Margaret and John Eales, Brenda Vallance and Marjorie Wicks.

(EALES COLLECTION)

that when Miss Manning had the shop, 'the news-paper train came through at about 5.30 in the morning and the papers were delivered to Manning's for 3s. a week on a two-wheeled hand trolley.'

When she came to retire she asked John Eales, who had taken over responsibility for the Sunday papers in 1969, if he would like to take on the dailies as well. John sold the Sundays from the Treasure Chest, the second-hand shop run by Mrs Pat Johnson and at the time of writing occupied by Gemini Video. So in 1975, John and Margaret Eales started South Brent News in what, in 2005, is the Mini-Market. Margaret tells us:

After three years the shop became too small for our stock. We then purchased the shop next door, now the Mare and Foal. Business was good, selling confectionery, toys, stationery, wool, haberdashery, books, maps and greetings cards, not forgetting newpapers and magazines. It was a friendly shop where people could come and have a chat and we often found ourselves listening to someone's troubles. My sister, Betty Vallance, Marjorie Wicks and Esther Warnes worked at the shop. We all worked together as a happy family although it was hard work and we worked long hours each day. We had great support from the village. We enjoyed 19 years of business. I look back with many memories and a lot of laughs.

Another of the successful enterprises in Brent is DIY store Wakeley's, which first opened in February 1978 on a six-month trial, South Hams District Council having waived shop rates for six months to give Fred and Ray Wakeley the chance to make the Station Yard shop a success. The Wakeley family had been established as builders in Brent since 1961. The store is now one of Brent's major assets, selling a wide range of DIY and housewares, gardening and pet supplies and footwear, as well as operating a hire centre for such items as cement mixers, carpet cleaners and small tools.

The Last Mill Closes – the End of Another Era

Manor Mills finally closed in 1992 after operating as a sawmill and timber yard for over 100 years. The Slumberland Co., who had taken over the mill in 1984 to make components for beds, blamed the closure on losses made since 1990, when it had become more cost-effective to buy-in components rather than making them in the factory. A total of 20 men and two women were made redundant, some of them with more than 40 years' service at the mill.

Yes or No to Shell?

In 1988 news broke that the petrol giant Royal Dutch Shell had plans to build a new motorway-style service station on the A38 between Wrangaton and South Brent. Their original proposal included a travel lodge, restaurant, picnic area and tourist information centre, along with parking for heavy goods vehicles, caravans and 80 cars. Plans to include a hotel were later dropped. The Dartmoor National Park turned down all of Shell's proposals on the grounds that land in the National Park should not be used for commercial development of this type. Shell appealed against the decision and a public inquiry launched at the beginning of August in the Village Hall went on for four days and was then adjourned. The enquiry was set to be reopened, this time in Ugborough Village Hall, in September 1989. Again the plans were opposed, not only by the National Park but also by two local groups, the South Brent Action and Community Group, under the chairmanship of Colonel Peter Lodge, and the South Brent and Lower Glaze Group, under the joint chairmanship of Paul Chester and Roger Webster.

The two groups were against the proposals for several reasons. They felt that the Dartmoor National Park should be protected against development that would harm the beauty of the landscape; that there was a possibility of pollution both of local water supplies and of the Glaze Brook itself, which remains an important river for breeding fish. There was concern over the possibility of noise, litter and 24-hour lighting on the site, and it was also felt that, with the Carew Service Station staying open all night, the development was not really necessary. The site in question was also considered to be hazardous, the distance between Wrangaton slip road and the entrance to the site, and between the exit from the site and the South Brent slip road, would be only half the minimum length between junctions required by the Department of Transport. An evening session of the enquiry on 3 August was attended by many local people, who agreed that this stretch of the road was already dangerous. Nearly 200 people wrote to the Department of the Environment to object to Shell's plans and proposals for a service station in the Brent area were finally dropped. The Carew Service Station still provides petrol and shop services to motorists, while the arguments about safety still rumble on.

Boundary Changes

In 1993 the electors of South Brent once again protested about being included in the Outer Plymouth area. Following boundary changes which saw the end of the Totnes Parliamentary Constituency, South Brent became part of South Hams, retaining its links with Totnes and the eastern end of the South Hams itself. Parliamentary reorganisation in 1993 saw the demise of the South Hams Parliamentary Constituency and its division into two, Totnes and South West Devon. During the consultation process it was proposed to substitute

Bere Ferrers, which was originally to be in the new South West Devon Constituency, with South Brent, taking Brent out of the Totnes Constituency. The Parish Council strongly objected to this move and the 2,181 electors were asked to sign a petition in support. The councillors themselves went out in force, collecting signatures at the street fair and knocking on doors in an effort to get at least 70 per cent of electors to sign. With over 1,300 signatures, Brent remained in the Totnes Parliamentary Constituency where historically it had always been.

The Lion of Brent

Brent made the national Press once again in November 1998, when a lion was spotted in the area. Wild cats sightings in the moorland areas of the South West were quite common in the 1990s, the most famous being the 'Beast of Bodmin'. Paul Gourley, of Cheston Farm Caravan Park, first spotted the lion whilst he was returning from taking his children, Terri and Shaun, to school. He described the animal as being in a poor state and running towards him. When he got to within about 15–20 yards of him, the lion, which was seen to have a bloody mane, went through a hedge and into a field. A paw print was found which experts considered to belong to a young lion of between 18 months and two years. Later that day, a builder working near Marley Head also reported seeing the lion. There was obvious

concern within the village and head teacher Mrs Helen Nicholls urged parents to be cautious in getting their children to and from the primary school.

Nine-year-old Douglas Everett of Quarry Park, determined to reassure people that there was nothing to worry about, asked his father, Richard Everett, to put his toy lion in the estate agency window with the message, 'Found in my bedroom'. Martin French and Paul Sparkes, of the Carew Service Station, raised a total of £500 for the 1998 BBC's Children in Need Appeal by dressing up as a lion for the day to raise money from their customers. Like other 'beasts' sighted over the years, it is not known where the animal came from. Although it has not been seen since, those who saw it are certain of what they saw.

Railway

In January 1994 it was reported that Devon County Council was investigating the possibility of reopening the station at Brent which had been closed some 30 years earlier. The concept, part of a long-term strategy to take pressure off the roads, had the full backing of local county councillor Mrs Cathy Pannell. The intention to reopen the station was repeated in the Dartmoor National Park Local Plan in 2003 when it was noted that, 'Proposals to establish new station facilities at South Brent will be permitted.' At the same time it was noted that

Although the station buildings are long gone, the main line to Penzance still runs through the site of Brent Station and steam enthusiasts get a good view of passing trains from the bridges. Here a double-headed train passes through the site of Brent Station, a reminder of the days when the station was in its heyday and such trains would have stopped.

(MILLER COLLECTION)

additional car-parking facilities would be needed and land at the end of the present car park was earmarked for such purposes.

A Very Lively Community

Brentonians are very fortunate in having many organisations and groups providing them with interests and activities.

Although mention has already been made of some of the older groups – SBADS, the Twinning Association, the Women's Institute, the Mothers' Union – over time other groups have been formed.

Women's Institute Again

At the annual meeting in November 1978 it was decided to have a trial year with six meetings in the afternoons (during the winter months), and six in the evenings. This was to encourage new and younger members as, with the growth of the village, many young people had moved into Brent, some with young children who could not be left in the afternoons and some who worked during the day. It was decided to hold the Christmas party on 9 December at 7.30p.m. and to make it an open meeting to welcome new members. In January 1979 18 new members were welcomed as a result of the party. It was then decided that, although many older members would not feel like turning out on winter evenings, as it was the evening meetings that had helped increase membership, future meetings would be held on the first Wednesday evening of the month.

In 1980 it was found that Mrs Elsie Preston, the only founder member still alive in the village, had ambitions to go for a once-in-a-lifetime helicopter ride. The efforts of the institute secretary resulted in the date being set for 17 July 1980 at Lympstone, unhappily called off at the last minute by the Royal Marines. Mrs Preston did, however, eventually have her wish fulfilled.

Brent Singers, including Andrew Parris, Alistair Cuthbertson, Mike Snelson, David Green, Paul Gibbons, Barry Rice, Darroll Angus, Richard Stevens, John Stanyon, Alf Young, Bryan Ostler, Alan Prince, Mike Roberts, Ray Burgess, Keith Laity, John Bryden, Kevin Mortimore, John Meesham, Jean Meesham, Janet Madge, Gill Taylor, Carole Mitchell, Juliet Harrison, Anne Billman, Stella Gillingham, Grace Dovell, Ursula Reid-Robertson, Anne Howson, Ann Laity, Felicity Summers, Chris Snelson, Jill Barber, Delia Sharpe, Margaret Hayward, Penny Johnson, Angela Mortimore, Cynthia Bird, Chris Hodson, Margaret Somerville, Eileen Bird, Jacqui Pulley, Julia Carroll, Andrea Larmour, Sylvia Frampton, Roland Mason (conductor) Rosalind Ramage, Jenny Prince, Sandy Baines, Ann Carter.

(BRENT SINGERS COLLECTION)

The Devon Wildlife Trust seat, installed at Ladyswood in 2004. Left to right back row: *Alan Baker, Rob Hamar, Celia Ralph, Don Evans, Grace and Richard Dovell;* front row: *Eileen Blockley, Margery Evans, Dawn Lenn from HQ with her son and Margery's dog, Oscar.* (Blockley Collection)

In 1982, when Rosemary Evans was first president, the WI branch had 75 members, a number which, in 2005, has halved. Life early in the twenty-first century has changed, and although the WI is no longer 'jam and Jerusalem', this change has affected other groups, as much as it has the WI.

In 1995, to commemorate the 75th anniversary of the Devon branch of the WI, a commemorative banner was carried from WI to WI across the county. It was brought from Buckfastleigh to South Brent by motorbike and sidecar, though probably the most unusual part of its journey was from South Brent to Bittaford by public service bus, accompanied by a farmer and his flock of chickens!

One of the more famous visitors to South Brent WI was Anna Wing, who played Lou Beale in the BBC soap 'Eastenders'. The actress, whose mother had been a life-long member of the WI, was on holiday in Devon and decided to look in on the coffee morning. She came in and chatted with the members and then did the draw.

Brent WI was part of the Anstice group of WIs which also included Ivybridge, The Erme, Sparkwell, Ermington, Cornwood and Lee Moor. In 1996 the group won both competition cups in the same year, one for handicrafts and one for produce (cookery).

The Women's Institute can always be relied upon for topical and ingenious entries into the Brent carnival. They even emulated other members of the Institute, appearing one year as the 'Calendar Girls'.

The Devon Wildlife Trust

Eileen Blockley and Barbara Lodge, both founder members of the local Devon Wildlife Group, here chart its history from its foundation:

With the help of the Totnes Group, the South Brent Group of the Devon Wildlife Trust came into being in October 1990 under the chairmanship of Robin Barnden. He gave a good start but sadly had to resign after a year. Our first event that October was a resounding success, with an audience of over 80, culminating in a presentation by Simon Roper on badgers. Since then the group has organised talks and walks nearly every month, has raised funds for the Devon Wildlife Trust (South Brent people are so generous) and generally worked to raise awareness of the work by the Trust.

In November 1994 we welcomed the first of the Ivybridge Group and amalgamated with them. That saved both groups – we could not have sustained our effort without their involvement as our committee was stretched.

Our informal planning meetings are held in private houses and we warmly welcome any interested participants. 'Nature notes' form an integral part, an unlikely

The Women's Institute

The visit of 'Eastenders' star Anna Wing to Brent WI. Left to right, back row: Ivy Sheppherd, Rosemary Evans, Wendy Woodley, Pauline Mitchell, Betty Skinner; middle row: Pauline Juste, Vera Bennett, Liz Riddick, Anna Wing, Doreen Puddifoot; front row: Mrs Stevens, ?, Ada Sparkes, Sylvia Warman, Lillian Hawes. (WI COLLECTION)

In 1996 the WI won both Anstice competition cups in the same year, one for handicrafts and one for produce. Left to right: Sylvia Warman, Pauline Juste and Maureen Grassby. (WI COLLECTION)

Brent Broilers wait for the bus to take the 75th anniversary banner of the Devon Federation of WIs to Bittaford. Left to right: Pam Honeywell, Inez Jordan, Wendy Woodley, Vera Bennett, Mrs Doreen Dover, Sylvia Warman, Stella Stickland, Betty Skinner, Esther Warnes, Rosemary Evans, Rosie Mallard and Pauline Juste. (WI COLLECTION)

The WI anniversary cake-cutting. Those pictured include: *Gill Taylor, Stella Stickland, Vera Bennett, Jenny Pike, Esther Warnes, Rosemary Evans, Doreen Puddefoot, Betty Skinner, Bernice Pike, Win O'Connor, Pauline Juste, Hilda Hard, Pam Hopkins, Vera Jordan, Gwen Trevennan, Joy Hayman, Wendy Woodley, Elizabeth Rush, Anne Bailey, Eve Stewart, Val Chalklin, Dulce Pearse, Mary Slade, Margaret Catt, Hazel Millington, Iris Hamlyn, Maureen Grassby, Sylvia Warman, Mrs Pollinger, Rosie Mullens, Peggy Johns, Inez Jordan.* (WI COLLECTION)

In 1990 the WI celebrated its 70th anniversary and entered the summer carnival in true WI style. From left to right: *Rosemary Evans, Wendy Woodley, Pauline Mitchell, Pauline Juste, Vera Bennett, Esther Warnes, Sylvia Warman, Stella Stickland and Sandra Thomas, with Betty Skinner pouring the champagne.*

(WI COLLECTION)

item on most committee agendas, and 'business' is kept to a minimum.

The seat in Ladyswood (the Trust's first nature reserve) was installed in 2004 in memory of one of our members.

Brent Singers

Founded in 1979, Brent Singers is a group from the local community united by the love of singing both sacred and secular music.

Major concerts have included: Bach's 'St John's Passion', Handel's 'Messiah', Hayden's 'Nelson Mass', Brahms' 'Requiem', Dvorak and Schubert Masses, Poulenc's 'Stabat Mater', Father Sebastian's 'Cantata for a New Era', the Faure, Durufle, Mozart and Rutter Requiems, Mozart's 'Coronation Mass', the Gounod 'St Cecilia Mass' and Vivaldi's 'Gloria'.

In addition, original works by local composers John Railton and Nicholas Marshall have been successfully performed, as well as a first performance by Dr Francis Jackson. Lighter, more traditional, melodies have also been sung, including selections by Gilbert and Sullivan, as well as many Christmas concerts.

Most concerts take place at South Brent venues, mainly St Petroc's Church and nearby Buckfast Abbey, and conductors have included Steve Wilson, Peter McMullen, Nicholas Marshall, Roland Mason and John Scarfe.

In July 1987 the first joint concert was held in France in the Breton village of Châteauneuf-du-faou, twinned with South Brent.. This has become a very successful venture, with biennial visits to Brittany and Devon.

Fund-raising is a continuous activity and the choir has made significant contributions to the Old School Community Centre, the Village Hall, the Health Centre, St Petroc's Church and the Children's Hospice Southwest in Bideford, as well as for the group itself.

Brent Island Trust

The Island at South Brent, in the present-day Dartmoor National Park, is a heritage site of regional importance.

The area where the River Avon divides as it flows past South Brent, running along both sides of the meadow, has always been known locally as 'The Island'. The Island, which has existed since the last ice age, is the meadowland nearest to the centre of Brent, an ancient, untouched area that has never been ploughed. As part of South Brent's industrial and social heritage, the weir, which powered two mills, one at nearby Millswood and the other half a mile away at Brent Mill, has been in existence since the seventeenth century. During that time it has created and sustained an important environment for wildlife. The weir is 40ft long and 7ft high, with a rim sloping 9ins from the Island side to the adjacent leat so that,

as the river rises and falls across it, the amount of water flowing into the leat is consistent. The weir, a fine example of stone engineering, is built of dressed granite; walling the banks and constructing half a mile of evenly sloped stone leat must have been an enormous task. For centuries it provided virtually free and constant power, and there are those who can remember the whole system in working order, with the leat cleaned every Saturday morning and the hatch gate opened and closed every day. The weir began to deteriorate when the Millswood mill burned down in 1948. The land was sold privately and the new owner, who neither lived in the village nor owned the weir, could not be expected to maintain it. Gradually it deteriorated, becoming a danger, particularly to children. The land came up for sale again in 1993 and the Brent Island Trust purchased The Island on 12 April 1994 for £26,500. The weir, with local help and a budget of £3,500, was repaired in the spring of 1995. However, on the night of New Year 2001, during an exceptional storm, the river rose 9ft, and huge boulders and tree trunks destroyed much of the good work of six years earlier.

As the weir area became extremely dangerous yet again the decision was made to restore it. With Faber Maunsell of Exeter as engineering consultants and contract overseers, and work carried out by contractors Southwest Highways of Exeter, this was successfully completed during the summer of 2003. The overall cost of the project was £44,000, paid for with funding from the Heritage Lottery Fund, the Environment Agency, Dartmoor National Park Authority, South Hams District and South Brent Parish Councils. There was tremendous support from the local community, which contributed a significant ten per cent of the total through donations, pledges, and many other local fund-raising initiatives. The leat was restored at the same time by employees of the Dartmoor National Park Authority.

The Linhay has also been restored and is a haven for birds, as well as being a focus for information and education. South Brent Primary School has given considerable support and has carried out many of its own surveys and other activities on The Island.

Professional and voluntary surveys have shown that species of flora and fauna are being maintained at a steady level. The safe passage and breeding in the River Avon of Atlantic salmon is encouraged and bats are breeding in the nearby Brunel railway arch and the Parish Church of St Petroc.

The Island is managed for people to freely enjoy and for the protection of wildlife within the immediate and wider environment, the aim being to maintain a complex of habitats in order to protect a wide variety of species for their benefit and for the whole community.

The Island is a significant part of community life in South Brent and remains a tranquil area of outstanding natural beauty. The tenth anniversary

Recent Pantomimes

Greg Wall, Cliff Bailey, Vincent McNevin, John Giles, John Ellison, Paul Wonnacott and Hamish Barclay as the dwarves in John Palmer's 1997 production of Snow White.
(MALE COLLECTION)

The cast of John Palmer's 2003 production of Cinderella including, standing: John Ellison, John Giles, Donna Warnes, Kim Kidney, Beth Goodey, Jessica Plummer, Robin Willoughby, Ron Akehurst, Sue Burgess, Paul Wonnacott, Rob Kidney, Tom Cuthbertson; kneeling: Grace Scott, Rose Willoughby, Al Thomas, Terri Gourley, Bea Chapman, Tori Plummer, Felix Jozsa, Shaun Gourley, Luke Chapman, Kate Scott.
(MALE COLLECTION)

Left: Jessica Plummer as Cinderella with ugly sisters Petula and Flatula, alias Greg Wall and John Giles.
(MALE COLLECTION)

Above: The 'pop-group', Sleeping Beauty, 2001. Left to right: Fairy Cake (Greg Wall), Evening Herald (Mark Atkins), Tickles the jester (John Giles), the King (Paul Wonnacott) and Fairy Nuff (Ron Akehurst).
(MALE COLLECTION)

The Sleeping Beauty, 2001, and cake-making with Annemarie Senior, Mike Roberts, Val Meek, John Giles and Mark Atkins.
(MALE COLLECTION)

of its purchase by the Brent Island Trust was celebrated with a fair on The Island on 6 June 2004.

The Old School
Community Centre

The 125th anniversary of South Brent Board School saw its official transformation from village school into a lifelong learning and community centre. The old school building served the children of South Brent until the opening of the new school in 1997, at which time South Brent Community Centre Group managed to buy the site with the help of loans and many fundraising activities. Major funding for the project came from the South West of England Regional Development Agency, a branch of the European Regional Development Fund, South Devon and Dartmoor Leader II, the Dartmoor National Park Authority, South Brent Parish Council, the Tudor Trust, the Garfield Weston, Lloyds TSB and Rank Foundations, and the Beatrice Laing and Viscount Amery's Trusts. The community centre, at the heart of the village, houses, among other things, the pre-school, the library and the church office and, along with Brent's other venues, is a centre for meetings and events.

PC Debbie Taylor.

Policing Today

PC Debbie Taylor, who was brought up in South Brent, describes her role in the town:

The principles of policing have not changed in many years. The technology may have been updated – we don't have to rely on the telephone kiosks in Fore Street or Exeter Road (although they do come in useful at times). Our current radio system is due to be updated with a more high-tech system later next year. This fills me with dread – I haven't mastered our neighbourhood beat manager's mobile phone yet!

Our horse has been upgraded to a four-wheel version, which still needs to be fed and watered in the form of servicing (more regularly than the average police vehicle, I hasten to add).

Although officers were thrilled when motor vehicles were introduced and bicycles were made redundant, bicycles have been given a dusting off and are seen on the streets in some areas of Devon and Cornwall. We at South Brent may be seen in the saddle in the future – watch this space.

The introduction of the Police and Criminal Evidence Act in 1984 has had a massive impact on the way we deal with offenders. Whilst many lament the passing of times, whether anecdotal or not, when the local bobby might have clipped someone around the ear, those days, if they ever existed, are definitely history. Society has changed significantly and policing styles evolve with that.

We keep ourselves fully equipped for those farmyard moments, a rural officer would never be far from his/her wellies, although we do get caught out at times – manure over the lace-ups is not a nice thing, especially if your next job is taking a crime report in the vicar's lounge.

More of our work is town/city type crimes exported to rural areas by travelling criminals. Although we have a very low crime rate, we are less likely to deal with sheep rustling or salmon poaching but with thefts from or of motor vehicles.

The police houses have more or less been sold, although they remain very identifiable as police houses, sometimes with the original colour scheme. Some officers still receive a non-increasing (or ring-fenced) rent allowance or a housing allowance. Officers joining the service today do not receive this monthly allowance and have not done so for more than 10 years.

Some things don't change – officers are still required to request permission to move house, get married or to co-habit.

We have moved on from truncheons – officers carry an extendable baton made of steel known as a 'Casco'. This item is more often used for breaking into cars or properties (with the consent of the owners, of course), rather than using force against our criminal fraternity.

The cape has been given to the Force Museum, officers now wear either a Gore-Tex jacket or a 'fleece' style jacket. We carry our other pieces of equipment in a garment that resembles a string vest. It's very bulky and is not conducive to running after offenders! Our uniform is not guaranteed for heavy rainfall as I have discovered on many occasions. It's unfortunate that South Brent is believed to have one of the heaviest rainfalls in Europe!

Officers have been known by many names, from 'Village Constable' through to 'Resident Officer' and 'Community Constable', 'Rural Beat Officer' to the present day 'Neighbourhood Beat Manager'.

Myself and my colleagues, PC Partridge and PC Hopper enjoy this very diverse role because we believe that we can make a difference to the quality of life for the residents of South Brent.

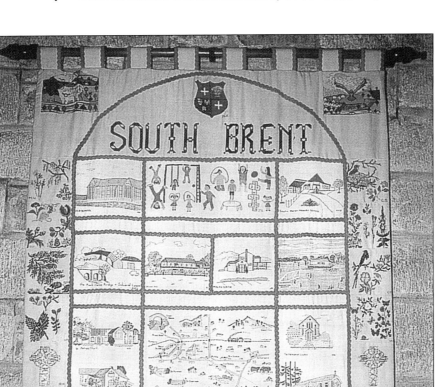

The Millennium Tapestry, which hangs in St Petroc's Church.   (MALE COLLECTION)

And So...

In the 2001 census South Brent had a population of 2,998. It is these people who make South Brent what it is. David Newman, a true Brentonian, remarks, 'There have been many wonderful characters who have stood outside the Anchor over the years.' Steve and Chris Hainsworth, who moved to the village after spending many happy holidays here, agree: 'South Brent to us and our friends is a little piece of Old England – clean, green and very friendly.' Alan Jones, who moved to South Brent after he married Chris in 1952, says, 'I wouldn't swap it for all the tea in China!', and Mary Jane, a more recent Brentonian, comments, 'It's so friendly and there's always something going on.' Frank Thompson, landlord of the Pack Horse, calls it 'a real village with real people'.

According to Paul and Lara Pennicotte-Henrie, 'It's not an archetype but a working village with a happy atmosphere, full of ordinary people.' Iris Petts considers it 'like having a second family', while Steve and Lynne Joyce, who run the fish and chip shop, say, 'It's fantastic and welcoming. We feel we've been here all our lives. It's a gentle, lovely place – like your warmest overcoat on a cold winter's day.'

In the year 2000 a tapestry was worked depicting South Brent in that special time in history. The rest of the portrait of South Brent is still being painted. As time and technology move on there will be more and more to write and record of those who live and work where the Avon leaves the bleak and dangerous southern Dartmoor heights and begins its journey through the tranquil South Hams, where a fortunate community lives and works in a fortunate place.

Subscribers

Ron Akehurst, South Brent
John Anderson and Annabel Saunders,
  Pleasantville, New York
Tom and Ann Anderson, Higher Downstow,
  South Brent
Jacqui, James and Nick Andrews
Julie Andrews, South Brent
Les Andrews and M. Jeal, South Brent
R.G. and D.J. Andrews, South Brent
William R. Andrews, Farmer
Bob and Susan Armstrong, Cayuga, Ontario,
  Canada
Mr and Mrs David Ayres
Sidney and Joan Ayres (née Cole)
Michael D. Baines, South Brent, Devon
The Barclay Family, Yonder Cross
Andrew and Elizabeth Bateman, Manor Court
Diana Bennett, Fleet, Hampshire
Eileen Blockly, South Brent, Devon
Mrs M. Bradford
E. and W. Brown, South Brent, Devon
P.R. and M.V. Brown, South Brent, Devon
Ray Brown, Lisburn, N. Ireland. Avon Dam
  1955–57
John and Ann, Richard, Sarah and Rosanna
  Buckpitt, Marley Thatch Farm, South Brent
Marilyn Bullen
K.J. Burrow, Bucks Cross, Devon
B.J. Burrows
Fred Burrows, South Brent
Ian Burrows
Richard D. Carroll, South Brent, Devon
E. and M. Catt
Kevin and Jan Chamberlain, South Brent
Cdr and Mrs G.C. Chapman, Lydia Bridge
E. Chapple, Ivybridge, Devon
F. Choak, South Brent, Devon
George W.P. Clay
Gerald and Jean Cleave
Anya Cockings, South Brent
David and Sheila Cockings
Neil Cockings, South Brent
John H. Collier, South Brent, Devon
Pamela Cornwell, Ivybridge, Devon
John Cranch, South Brent
Shaun and Judith Crannis, South Brent

Peter and Maureen Crimp, South Brent, Devon
Gary Crosbie, Leighton Buzzard, Hertforshire
Kevin Crosbie, Trowbridge, Wiltshire
Mrs Pat Crosbie
Alastair and Margaret Cuthbertson, South
  Brent, Devon
A. and K. Dahill, South Brent
Evan and Anthea Davies, South Brent
Brian and Lyn Dent, Avonwick
James Dent
Sarah Dent
A. and C. Doree, The Royal Oak, South Brent
Margaret Eales, South Brent
John and Shirley Eatwell, South Brent, Devon
Emily J. Edginton
Lucie K. Edginton
Paul and Caroline Edginton, South Brent
W.J. Edmunds, Gribblesdown, South Brent
The Elwell Family
Angela J. Endean, Totnes, Devon
Bill and Wendy Evemy, South Brent
Dick, Mardie, Romilly, Henry, Douglas Everett
Tim and Felicity Ferry, South Brent
A. and J. Field, Plymouth, Devon
A.H. and B.E. Field, South Brent, Devon
K. and S. Field, Torquay
Peter and Katie Finch, Cyprus
Godfrey H. Foot and Margaret C. Foot (née
  Cranch), Kingskerswell, South Devon
The Ford Family, Rock Cottage, Lydia Bridge
M. Froom, Ugborough, Devon
Ben and Stella Gillingham, Bridge House,
  Didworthy, South Brent
David Goss, Swindon, Wiltshire. Formerly
  South Brent
Jan and Mike Goss, South Brent, Devon
H.P. Greenwood
Mr Derek Grills, South Brent, Devon
Mr Keith Grills, South Brent, Devon
N. Gubbin, Brentonian
Christine Hainsworth
Mandy and Tim Haley, South Brent, Devon
Angela and Denis Hall, South Brent
Michael Hall
Christine Halstead, Riverside, South Brent
Revd Derek and Hennie Hamblin, South Brent

Rupert and Cordelia Hancock, South Brent
Lester and Tina Hard, Wrangaton, South Brent
C. and J. Harwood, Wrangaton
Peter Hawken MBE, Plymouth, and Mrs D. Hawken (née Preston)
Bill and Joy Hayman (née Lang), South Brent
Harry and Doris Hill, South Brent
Valerie and Dennis Hoare, South Brent, Devon
Honeywill, South Brent
Pam Honeywill (née Smith),
Edward, Gregory, Delvinya, Tracy and David Howard
Phill and Rachel Howing-Nicholls, South Brent
Joyce and Ralph Howitt, South Brent
Briant T. Hughes
Eileen M. Hull, South Brent, Devon
Sophia E.D. Jackson
Harry and Barbara Jane, South Brent, Devon
Shelagh and Graham Jeffreys, South Brent
Joan and Peter Jenkins, South Brent
Peggy and Johnny John
M. Johnson, Webland
Ann Jones, South Brent, Devon
Mr A.T. Jones, South Brent
Alan T. Jones
Vera Jordan, South Brent, Devon
The Jozsa Family, Aish, South Brent
The Karkeek Family
Ann Kelly, Wesley Barn, South Brent, Devon
Avril and Peter Kelly
Bill Kennard
Mr and Mrs A. Ketteringham
Graham V. Korner
Ray and Lorna Lane (née Lang), Gwent
Bernard and Mandy Langdon
D.A. Langdon, Pershore, Worcester
G.E. and R.J. Langdon, Pershore, Worcester
Tim and Jane Lankester
Brian and Liz Lavers, South Brent, Devon
Barbara Lodge, South Brent, Devon
E.S. and R.C. Luscombe
Mr and Mrs T.H. Maddock
Mr B. Male, Totnes
Edgar George 'Eggie' Male, South Brent, Devon
Lilian Male, South Brent, Devon
Mrs Lillian Male, South Brent, Devon
Mr M. Male
R.A. and H.A. Male, South Brent
Elizabeth and Bob March, Ivybridge, Devon
Mona Marshall (née Lang), Reading
L. Mayling and V. Llewellyn, South Brent
Elizabeth McGuffog, Shaugh Prior
Vincent and Irene McNevin, Didworthy

John and Margaret Mead, South Brent
Christopher and Sally Merriman, Bristol
Malcolm, Bethan and Louise Merriman, South Brent
Jean and Peter Miller
Hazel Millington, Western Australia
Hazel E. Millington, Hillside, South Brent
Edward and Shirley Mitchell, Paignton
James A. Mitchell, North Huish, Devon
Pauline E. Mitchell, South Brent, Devon
Mrs L. Moore, South Brent
Peter and Pearl Moore
The Morris Family, Hillside, South Brent
Mrs Sheila Morrish and Family, South Brent
David J. Mould, South Brent, Devon
Ray Mugridge
Kay and Patrick Mullen, Ivybridge, Devon
Jennifer Mumford (née Jonas)
Richard A. Mumford, South Brent, Devon
Ginny Murgatroyd, South Brent
D.G. Newman, South Brent
E.V. Newman, South Brent, Devon
Kenneth Newman
Mr Trevor Newman, South Brent, Devon
Jeremy Niblett, Bahrain
Revd David and Mrs Elisabeth Niblett, Glastonbury
Frank and Ruth Noble, Old Didworthy Farm
Joyce and Mossy O'Connell
Old School Centre Library, South Brent
Stuart D. Orr Esq, Great Palstone, South Brent
Mrs Ann Packman (Luscombe), Oxford
Norman Perkins, South Brent
Colin R. Perry, South Brent, Devon
Brenda Perryman, Bovey Tracey, Devon
Jenny Pike, South Brent
Gaynor and Adrian Platt, South Brent, Devon
John and Jill Poulton, Torquay
Diane and John Reed, South Brent
U.A. Reid-Robertson
Miss Agnes R. Rivers-Moore, Canada
D. Mark Rivers-Moore, Redhill, Surrey
Mike Roberts
Dulce Robertson, South Brent, Devon
Monty Rogers, formerly of Aish
M. and M. Roper, Plymouth, Devon
Anthony Roper
Cathy Ross, South Brent
Gillian Ross, South Brent
Phyllis D. Rundle, South Brent
Elizabeth N. Rush
Michael and Jean Sandry, South Brent
Robert Savery, South Brent

Mrs C. Scott, Horsebrook
John Shepherd, South Brent, Devon
Philip Sheppard, Didworthy, South Brent, Devon
S.B. Shillabeer, South Brent, Devon
Mark Simmons, Cornwall
Frank and Joyce Sings, South Brent
Kathy and Tim Sings, South Brent
Pamela and Sarah Sitton, Morgana Cottage, South Brent
Edgar John Skelton, Avonwick
Edward Skelton
Betty Margaret Skinner
David and Sarah Smith, South Brent
Miss Charlotte Soby, South Brent, Devon
Dorothea Solomon (née Hayman), Ivybridge, Devon
John Soper, South Brent, Devon
L. Soper, South Brent, Devon
Mark and Sharon Soper, Brakefield, South Brent
South Brent Parish Council
Frances Eileen Sparkes
W. May Sparkes, South Brent, Devon
Rev. Canon John and Mrs Spence, South Brent
Don and Rosemary Stanbury
Margie and Peter Stevens, South Brent, Devon
Richard Stevens, South Brent, Devon
Eva B. Stewart, South Brent
Pat and Duncan Stewart, South Brent
John and Felicity Summers, Aish, South Brent
Syon Abbey, South Brent
Brian Thomas, Clobells, South Brent
Dr Elfyn Thomas, South Brent
The Thompsons, The Packhorse
Roderick Thomson, South Brent
D. and Tina Tomlin
Neil Toogood
Jane Tuson, South Brent

Eric and Nolene Uren, Australia
Betty C. Vallance, South Brent, Devon
Colin J. Vallance, South Brent, Devon
John and Kim Van Der Kiste, South Brent, Devon
Kate Van Der Kiste, South Brent
Kevin Vickers, South Brent, Devon
Mrs V. Vincent, Portesham, Dorchester, Dorset
Mr and Mrs Peter Wakeham, Rattery, South Brent
Raymond F. Wakeley, South Brent, Devon
Stephen R. Wakeley, South Brent, Devon
John F.W. Walling, Newton Abbot, Devon
John D. Warman, South Brent, Devon
Miss Donna L. Warne, South Brent, Devon
Ann Warren, Lutton, South Brent
Zoe Warren
Webber, South Brent
John and Sara Weymouth, South Brent
Carole Whittard (née Goss), Frome, Somerset. Formerly South Brent
Paul Widdicombe, Clarence House, South Brent
James Wiggam, Cheshunt, Hertfordshire
Sally Wiggam, Taunton, Somerset
Sue and Ivan Wiggam, Bradford on Avon, Wiltshire
David Wild, South Brent
John E. Wild
Elise R. Willisson, South Brent, Devon
Revd David R. Winnington-Ingram, Vicar of South Brent, Devon
Brian and Val Wollington, South Brent, Devon
Gary M. Wonnacott, South Brent, Devon
Paul and Mary Wonnacott, South Brent
Clive and Nano Wood (née O'Connell),
Mark and Dawn Woodhouse, South Brent
Malcolm and Cindy Wright, Totnes, Devon
Michael and Stella Wright (née Manning), Stoke Poges

There are now over 140 titles in the Community History Series.

For a full listing of these and other Halsgrove publications, please visit www.halsgrove.co.uk or telephone 01884 243 242.

In order to include as many historical photographs as possible in this volume, a printed index is not included. However, the Devon titles in the Community History Series are indexed by Genuki.

For further information and indexes to various volumes in the series, please visit: http://www.cs.ncl.ac.uk/genuki/DEV/indexingproject.html